# CAPE COD

AUTHOR:
HENRY D. THOREAU

ILLUSTRATOR:
CLIFTON JOHNSON

# Contents

I  THE SHIPWRECK ............................................................................1
II  STAGE COACH VIEWS ...............................................................13
III  THE PLAINS OF NAUSET ..........................................................24
IV  THE BEACH .................................................................................45
V  THE WELLFLEET OYSTERMAN ...............................................62
VI  THE BEACH AGAIN ....................................................................80
VII  ACROSS THE CAPE ..................................................................101
VIII  THE HIGHLAND LIGHT ...........................................................118
IX  THE SEA AND THE DESERT ...................................................139
X  PROVINCETOWN ......................................................................167
APPENDIX ........................................................................................213
    PLOT SUMMARY ........................................................................214
    HISTORICAL CONTEXT ............................................................216
    BIOGRAPHY ................................................................................218

# I

## THE SHIPWRECK

Wishing to get a better view than I had yet had of the ocean, which, we are told, covers more than two-thirds of the globe, but of which a man who lives a few miles inland may never see any trace, more than of another world, I made a visit to Cape Cod in October, 1849, another the succeeding June, and another to Truro in July, 1855; the first and last time with a single companion, the second time alone. I have spent, in all, about three weeks on the Cape; walked from Eastham to Province-town twice on the Atlantic side, and once on the Bay side also, excepting four or five miles, and crossed the Cape half a dozen times on my way; but having come so fresh to the sea, I have got but little salted. My readers must expect only so much saltness as the land breeze acquires from blowing over an arm of the sea, or is tasted on the windows and the bark of trees twenty miles inland, after September gales. I have been accustomed to make excursions to the ponds within ten miles of Concord, but latterly I have extended my excursions to the seashore.

I did not see why I might not make a book on Cape Cod, as well as my neighbor on "Human Culture." It is but another name for the same thing, and hardly a sandier phase of it. As for my title, I suppose that the word Cape is from the French *cap*; which is from the Latin *caput*, a head; which is, perhaps, from the verb *capere*, to take,—that being the part by which we take hold of a thing:—Take Time by the forelock. It is also the safest part to take a serpent by. And as for Cod, that was derived directly from that "great store of codfish" which Captain Bartholomew Gosnold caught there in 1602; which fish appears to have been so called from the Saxon word *codde*, "a case in which seeds are lodged," either from the form of the fish, or the quantity of spawn it contains; whence also, perhaps, *codling* (*pomum coctile?*) and coddle,—to cook green like peas. (V. Dic.)

Cape Cod is the bared and bended arm of Massachusetts: the shoulder is at Buzzard's Bay; the elbow, or crazy-bone, at Cape Mallebarre; the wrist at Truro; and the sandy fist at Provincetown,—behind which the State stands on her guard, with her back to the Green Mountains, and her feet planted on the floor of the ocean, like an athlete protecting her Bay,—boxing with northeast storms, and, ever and anon, heaving up her Atlantic adversary from the lap of earth,—ready to thrust forward her other fist, which keeps guard the while upon her breast at Cape Ann.

On studying the map, I saw that there must be an uninterrupted beach on the east or outside of the forearm of the Cape, more than thirty miles from the general line of the coast, which would afford a good sea view, but that, on account of an opening in the beach, forming the entrance to Nauset Harbor, in Orleans, I must strike it in Eastham, if I approached it by land, and probably I could walk thence straight to Race Point, about twenty-eight miles, and not meet with any obstruction.

We left Concord, Massachusetts, on Tuesday, October 9th, 1849. On reaching Boston, we found that the Provincetown steamer, which should have got in the day before, had not yet arrived, on account of a violent storm; and, as we noticed in the streets a handbill headed, "Death! one hundred and forty-five lives lost at Cohasset," we decided to go by way of Cohasset. We found many Irish in the cars, going to identify bodies and to sympathize with the survivors, and also to attend the funeral which was to take place in the afternoon;—and when we arrived at Cohasset, it appeared that nearly all the passengers were bound for the beach, which was about a mile distant, and many other persons were flocking in from the neighboring country. There were several hundreds of them streaming off over Cohasset common in that direction, some on foot and some in wagons,—and among them were some sportsmen in their hunting-jackets, with their guns, and game-bags, and dogs. As we passed the graveyard we saw a large hole, like a cellar, freshly dug there, and, just before reaching the shore, by a pleasantly winding and rocky road, we met several hay-riggings and farm-wagons coming away toward the meeting-house, each loaded with three large, rough deal boxes. We did not need to ask what was in them. The owners of the wagons were made the undertakers. Many horses in carriages were fastened to the fences near the shore, and, for a mile or more, up and down, the beach was covered with people looking out for bodies, and examining the fragments of the wreck. There was a small island called Brook Island, with a hut on it, lying just off the shore. This is said to be the rockiest shore in Massachusetts, from Nantasket to Scituate,—hard sienitic rocks, which the waves have laid bare, but have not been able to crumble. It has been the scene of many a shipwreck.

The brig *St. John*, from Galway, Ireland, laden with emigrants, was wrecked on Sunday morning; it was now Tuesday morning, and the sea was still breaking violently on the rocks. There were eighteen or twenty of the same large boxes that I have mentioned, lying on a green hillside, a few rods from the water, and surrounded by a crowd. The bodies which had been recovered, twenty-seven or eight in all, had been collected there. Some were rapidly nailing down the lids, others were carting the boxes away, and others were lifting the lids, which were yet loose, and peeping under the cloths, for each body, with such rags as still adhered to it, was covered loosely with a white sheet. I witnessed no signs of grief, but there was a sober dispatch of business which was affecting. One man was seeking to identify a particular body, and one undertaker or carpenter was calling to another to know in what box a certain child was put. I saw many marble feet and matted heads as the cloths were raised, and one livid, swollen, and mangled body of a drowned girl,—who probably had intended to go out to service in some American family,—to which some rags still adhered, with a string, half concealed by the flesh, about its swollen neck; the coiled-up wreck of a human hulk, gashed by the rocks or fishes, so that the bone and muscle were exposed, but quite bloodless,—merely red and white,—with wide-open and staring eyes, yet lustreless, dead-lights; or like the cabin windows of a stranded vessel, filled with sand. Sometimes there were two or more children, or a parent and child, in the same box, and on the lid would perhaps be written with red chalk, "Bridget such-a-one, and sister's child." The surrounding sward was covered with bits of sails and clothing. I have since heard, from one who lives by this beach, that a woman who had come over before, but had left her infant behind for her sister to bring, came and looked into these boxes and saw in one,—probably the same whose superscription I have quoted,—her child in her sister's arms, as if the sister had meant to be found thus; and within three days after, the mother died from the effect of that sight.

We turned from this and walked along the rocky shore. In the first cove were strewn what seemed the fragments of a vessel, in small pieces mixed with sand and sea-weed, and great quantities of feathers; but it looked so old and rusty, that I at first took it to be some old wreck which had lain there many years. I even thought of Captain Kidd, and that the feathers were those which sea-fowl had cast there; and perhaps there might be some tradition about it in the neighborhood. I asked a sailor if that was the *St. John*. He said it was. I asked him where she struck. He pointed to a rock in front of us, a mile from the shore, called the Grampus Rock, and added:

"You can see a part of her now sticking up; it looks like a small boat."

I saw it. It was thought to be held by the chain-cables and the anchors. I asked if the bodies which I saw were all that were drowned.

"Not a quarter of them," said he.

"Where are the rest?"

"Most of them right underneath that piece you see."

It appeared to us that there was enough rubbish to make the wreck of a large vessel in this cove alone, and that it would take many days to cart it off. It was several feet deep, and here and there was a bonnet or a jacket on it. In the very midst of the crowd about this wreck, there were men with carts busily collecting the sea-weed which the storm had cast up, and conveying it beyond the reach of the tide, though they were often obliged to separate fragments of clothing from it, and they might at any moment have found a human body under it. Drown who might, they did not forget that this weed was a valuable manure. This shipwreck had not produced a visible vibration in the fabric of society.

About a mile south we could see, rising above the rocks, the masts of the British brig which the *St. John* had endeavored to follow, which had slipped her cables and, by good luck, run into the mouth of Cohasset Harbor. A little further along the shore we saw a man's clothes on a rock; further, a woman's scarf, a gown, a straw bonnet, the brig's caboose, and one of her masts high and dry, broken into several pieces. In another rocky cove, several rods from the water, and behind rocks twenty feet high, lay a part of one side of the vessel, still hanging together. It was, perhaps, forty feet long, by fourteen wide. I was even more surprised at the power of the waves, exhibited on this shattered fragment, than I had been at the sight of the smaller fragments before. The largest timbers and iron braces were broken superfluously, and I saw that no material could withstand the power of the waves; that iron must go to pieces in such a case, and an iron vessel would be cracked up like an egg-shell on the rocks. Some of these timbers, however, were so rotten that I could almost thrust my umbrella through them. They told us that some were saved on this piece, and also showed where the sea had heaved it into this cove, which was now dry. When I saw where it had come in, and in what condition, I wondered that any had been saved on it. A little further on a crowd of men was collected around the mate of the *St. John*, who was telling his story. He was a slim-looking youth, who spoke of the captain as the master, and seemed a little excited. He was saying that when they jumped into the boat, she filled, and, the vessel lurching, the weight of the water in the boat caused the painter to break, and so they were separated. Whereat one man came away, saying:—

"Well, I don't see but he tells a straight story enough. You see, the weight of the water in the boat broke the painter. A boat full of water is very heavy,"—and so on, in a loud and impertinently earnest tone, as if he had a bet depending on it, but had no humane interest in the matter.

Another, a large man, stood near by upon a rock, gazing into the sea, and chewing large quids of tobacco, as if that habit were forever confirmed with him.

"Come," says another to his companion, "let's be off. We've seen the whole of it. It's no use to stay to the funeral."

Further, we saw one standing upon a rock, who, we were told, was one that was saved. He was a sober-looking man, dressed in a jacket and gray pantaloons, with his hands in the pockets. I asked him a few questions, which he answered; but he seemed unwilling to talk about it, and soon walked away. By his side stood one of the life-boatmen, in an oil-cloth jacket, who told us how they went to the relief of the British brig, thinking that the boat of the *St. John*, which they passed on the way, held all her crew,—for the waves prevented their seeing those who were on the vessel, though they might have saved some had they known there were any there. A little further was the flag of the *St. John* spread on a rock to dry, and held down by stones at the corners. This frail, but essential and significant portion of the vessel, which had so long been the sport of the winds, was sure to reach the shore. There were one or two houses visible from these rocks, in which were some of the survivors recovering from the shock which their bodies and minds had sustained. One was not expected to live.

We kept on down the shore as far as a promontory called Whitehead, that we might see more of the Cohasset Rocks. In a little cove, within half a mile, there were an old man and his son collecting, with their team, the sea-weed which that fatal storm had cast up, as serenely employed as if there had never been a wreck in the world, though they were within sight of the Grampus Rock, on which the *St. John* had struck. The old man had heard that there was a wreck, and knew most of the particulars, but he said that he had not been up there since it happened. It was the wrecked weed that concerned him most, rock-weed, kelp, and sea-weed, as he named them, which he carted to his barn-yard; and those bodies were to him but other weeds which the tide cast up, but which were of no use to him. We afterwards came to the life-boat in its harbor, waiting for another emergency,—and in the afternoon we saw the funeral procession at a distance, at the head of which walked the captain with the other survivors.

On the whole, it was not so impressive a scene as I might have expected. If I had found one body cast upon the beach in some lonely place, it would have affected me more. I sympathized rather with the winds and waves, as if to toss and mangle these poor human bodies was the order of the day. If this was the law of Nature, why waste any time in awe or pity? If the last day were come, we should not think so much about the separation of friends or the blighted prospects of individuals. I saw that corpses might be multiplied, as on the field of battle, till they no longer affected us in any degree, as exceptions to the common lot of humanity. Take all the graveyards together, they are always the majority. It is the individual and private that demands our sympathy. A man can attend but one funeral in the course of his life, can behold but one corpse. Yet I saw that the inhabitants of the shore would be not a little affected by this event. They would watch there many days and nights for the sea to give up its dead, and their imaginations and sympathies would supply the place of mourners far away, who as yet knew not of the wreck. Many days after this, something white was seen floating on the water by one who was sauntering on the beach. It was approached in a boat, and found to be the body of a woman, which had risen in an upright position, whose white cap was blown back with the wind. I saw that the beauty of the shore itself was wrecked for many a lonely walker there, until he could perceive, at last, how its beauty was enhanced by wrecks like this, and it acquired thus a rarer and sublimer beauty still.

Cohasset—The little cove at Whitehead promontory

Why care for these dead bodies? They really have no friends but the worms or fishes. Their owners were coming to the New World, as Columbus and the Pilgrims did,—they were within a mile of its shores; but, before they could reach it, they emigrated to a newer world than ever Columbus dreamed of, yet one of whose existence we believe that there is far more universal and convincing evidence—though it has not yet been discovered by science—than Columbus had of this; not merely mariners' tales and some paltry drift-wood and sea-weed, but a continual drift and instinct to all our shores. I saw their empty hulks that came to land; but they themselves, meanwhile, were cast upon some shore yet further west, toward which we are all tending, and which we shall reach at last, it may be through storm and darkness, as they did. No doubt, we have reason to thank God that they have not been "shipwrecked into life again." The mariner who makes the safest port in Heaven, perchance, seems to his friends on earth to be shipwrecked, for they deem Boston Harbor the better place; though perhaps invisible to them, a skillful pilot comes to meet him, and the fairest and balmiest gales blow off that coast, his good ship makes the land in halcyon days, and he kisses the shore in rapture there, while his old hulk tosses in the surf here. It is hard to part with one's body, but, no doubt, it is easy enough to do without it when once it is gone. All their plans and hopes burst like a bubble! Infants by the score dashed on the rocks by the enraged Atlantic Ocean! No, no! If the *St. John* did not make her port here, she has been telegraphed there. The strongest wind cannot stagger a Spirit; it is a Spirit's breath. A just man's purpose cannot be split on any Grampus or material rock, but itself will split rocks till it succeeds.

The verses addressed to Columbus, dying, may, with slight alterations, be applied to the passengers of the *St. John:*—

>"Soon with them will all be over,
>Soon the voyage will be begun
>That shall bear them to discover,
>Far away, a land unknown.
>
>"Land that each, alone, must visit,
>But no tidings bring to men;
>For no sailor, once departed,
>Ever hath returned again.
>
>"No carved wood, no broken branches,
>Ever drift from that far wild;
>He who on that ocean launches
>Meets no corse of angel child.
>
>"Undismayed, my noble sailors,
>Spread, then spread your canvas out;
>Spirits! on a sea of ether
>Soon shall ye serenely float!
>
>"Where the deep no plummet soundeth,
>Fear no hidden breakers there,
>And the fanning wing of angels

Shall your bark right onward bear.

"Quit, now, full of heart and comfort,
These rude shores, they are of earth;
Where the rosy clouds are parting,
There the blessed isles loom forth."

One summer day, since this, I came this way, on foot, along the shore from Boston. It was so warm that some horses had climbed to the very top of the ramparts of the old fort at Hull, where there was hardly room to turn round, for the sake of the breeze. The *Datura stramonium*, or thorn-apple, was in full bloom along the beach; and, at sight of this cosmopolite,—this Captain Cook among plants,—carried in ballast all over the world, I felt as if I were on the highway of nations. Say, rather, this Viking, king of the Bays, for it is not an innocent plant; it suggests not merely commerce, but its attend-ant vices, as if its fibres were the stuff of which pirates spin their yarns. I heard the voices of men shouting aboard a vessel, half a mile from the shore, which sounded as if they were in a barn in the country, they being between the sails. It was a purely rural sound. As I looked over the water, I saw the isles rapidly wasting away, the sea nibbling voraciously at the continent, the springing arch of a hill suddenly interrupted, as at Point Alderton,—what botanists might call premorse,—showing, by its curve against the sky, how much space it must have occupied, where now was water only, On the other hand, these wrecks of isles were being fancifully arranged into new shores, as at Hog Island, inside of Hull, where everything seemed to be gently lapsing, into futurity. This isle had got the very form of a ripple,—and I thought that the inhabitants should bear a ripple for device on their shields, a wave passing over them, with the *datura*, which is said to produce mental alienation of long duration without affecting the bodily health,[1] springing from its edge. The most interesting thing which I heard of, in this township of Hull, was an unfailing spring, whose locality was pointed out to me, on the side of a distant hill, as I was panting along the shore, though I did not visit it. Perhaps, if I should go through Rome, it would be some spring on the Capitoline Hill I should remember the longest. It is true, I was somewhat interested in the well at the old French fort, which was said to be ninety feet deep, with a cannon at the bottom of it. On Nantasket beach I counted a dozen chaises from the public-house. From time to time the riders turned their horses toward the sea, standing in the water for the coolness,—and I saw the value of beaches to cities for the sea breeze and the bath.

At Jerusalem village the inhabitants were collecting in haste, before a thunder-shower now approaching, the Irish moss which they had spread to dry. The shower passed on one side, and gave me a few drops only, which did not cool the air. I merely felt a puff upon my cheek, though, within sight, a vessel was capsized in the bay, and several others dragged their anchors, and were near going ashore. The sea-bathing at Cohasset Rocks was perfect. The water was purer and more transparent than any I had ever seen. There was not a particle of mud or slime about it. The bottom being sandy, I could see the sea-perch swimming about. The smooth and fantastically worn rocks, and the perfectly clean and tress-like rock-weeds falling over you, and attached so firmly to the rocks that you could pull yourself up by them, greatly enhanced the luxury of the bath. The stripe of barnacles just above the weeds reminded me of some vegetable growth,—the buds, and petals, and seed-vessels of flowers. They lay along the seams of the rock like buttons on a waistcoat. It was one of the hottest days in the year, yet I found the water so icy cold that I could swim but a stroke or two, and thought that, in case of shipwreck, there would be more danger of being chilled to death than simply drowned. One immersion was enough to make you forget the dog-days utterly. Though you were sweltering before, it will take you half an hour now to remember that it was ever warm. There were the tawny rocks, like lions couchant, defying the ocean, whose waves incessantly dashed against and scoured them with vast quantities of gravel. The water held in their little hollows, on the receding of the tide, was so crystalline that I could not believe it salt, but wished to drink it; and higher up were basins of fresh water left by the rain,—all which, being also of different depths and temperature, were convenient for different kinds of baths. Also, the larger hollows in the smoothed rocks formed the most convenient of seats and dressing-rooms. In these respects it was the most perfect seashore that I had seen.

I saw in Cohasset, separated from the sea only by a narrow beach, a handsome but shallow lake of some four hundred acres, which, I was told, the sea had tossed over the beach in a great storm in the spring, and, after the alewives had passed into it, it had stopped up its outlet, and now the alewives were dying: by thousands, and the inhabitants were apprehending a pestilence as the water evaporated. It had live rocky islets in it.

This Rock shore is called Pleasant Cove, on some maps; on the map of Cohasset, that name appears to be confined to the particular cove where I saw the wreck of the St. J aim. The ocean did not look, now, as if any were ever shipwrecked in it; it was not grand and sub-lime, but beautiful as a lake. Not a vestige of a wreck was visible, nor could I believe that the bones of many a shipwrecked man were buried in that pure sand. But to go on with our first excursion.

> [1] The Jamestown weed (or thorn-apple). "This, being an early plant, was gathered very young for a boiled salad, by some of the soldiers sent thither [*i.e.* to Virginia] to quell the rebellion of Bacon; and some of them ate plentifully of it, the effect of which was a very pleasant comedy, for they turned natural fools upon it for several days: one would blow up a feather in the air; another would dart straws at it with much fury; and another, stark naked, was sitting up in a corner like a monkey, grinning and making mows at them; a fourth would fondly kiss and paw his companions, and sneer in their faces, with a countenance more antic than any in a Dutch droll. In this frantic condition they were confined, lest they should, in their folly, destroy themselves,—though it was observed that all their actions were full of innocence and good

nature. Indeed, they were not very cleanly. A thousand such simple tricks they played, and after eleven days returned to themselves again, not remembering anything that had passed."—Beverly's *History of Virginia*, p. 120.

## II

### STAGE COACH VIEWS

After spending the night in Bridgewater, and picking up a few arrow-heads there in the morning, we took the cars for Sandwich, where we arrived before noon. This was the terminus of the "Cape Cod Railroad," though it is but the beginning of the Cape. As it rained hard, with driving mists, and there was no sign of its holding up, we here took that almost obsolete conveyance, the stage, for "as far as it went that day," as we told the driver. We had for-gotten how far a stage could go in a day, but we were told that the Cape roads were very "heavy," though they added that, being of sand, the rain would improve them. This coach was an exceedingly narrow one, but as there was a slight spherical excess over two on a seat, the driver waited till nine passengers had got in, without taking the measure of any of them, and then shut the door after two or three ineffectual slams, as if the fault were all in the hinges or the latch,—while we timed our inspirations and expirations so as to assist him.

We were now fairly on the Cape, which extends from Sandwich eastward thirty-five miles, and thence north and northwest thirty more, in all sixty-five, and has an average breadth of about five miles. In the interior it rises to the height of two hundred, and sometimes perhaps three hundred feet above the level of the sea. According to Hitchcock, the geologist of the State, it is composed almost entirely of sand, even to the depth of three hundred feet in some places, though there is probably a concealed core of rock a little beneath the surface, and it is of diluvian origin, excepting a small portion at the extremity and elsewhere along the shores, which is alluvial. For the first half of the Cape large blocks of stone are found, here and there, mixed with the sand, but for the last thirty miles boulders, or even gravel, are rarely met with. Hitchcock conjectures that the ocean has, in course of time, eaten out Boston, Harbor and other bays in the mainland, and that the minute fragments have been deposited by the currents at a distance from the shore, and formed this sand-bank. Above the sand, if the surface is subjected to agricultural tests, there is found to be a thin layer of soil gradually diminishing from Barnstable to Truro, where it ceases; but there are many holes and rents in this weather-beaten garment not likely to be stitched in time, which reveal the naked flesh of the Cape, and its extremity is completely bare.

I at once got out my book, the eighth volume of the Collections of the Massachusetts Historical Society, printed in 1802, which contains some short notices of the Cape towns, and began to read up to where I was, for in the cars I could not read as fast as I travelled. To those who came from the side of Plymouth, it said: "After riding through a body of woods, twelve miles in extent, interspersed with but few houses, the settlement of Sandwich appears, with a more agreeable effect, to the eye of the traveller." Another writer speaks of this as a *beautiful* village. But I think that our villages will bear to be contrasted only with one another, not with Nature. I have no great respect for the writer's taste, who talks easily about beautiful villages, embellished, perchance, with a "fulling-mill," "a handsome academy," or meeting-house, and "a number of shops for the different mechanic arts"; where the green and white houses of the gentry, drawn up in rows, front on a street of which it would be difficult to tell whether it is most like a desert or a long stable-yard. Such spots can be beautiful only to the weary traveller, or the returning native,—or, perchance, the repentant misanthrope; not to him who, with unprejudiced senses, has just come out of the woods, and approaches one of them, by a bare road, through a succession of straggling homesteads where he cannot tell which is the alms-house. However, as for Sandwich, I cannot speak particularly. Ours was but half a Sandwich at most, and that must have fallen on the buttered side some time. I only saw that it was a closely built town for a small one, with glass-works to improve its sand, and narrow streets in which we turned round and round till we could not tell which way we were going, and the rain came in, first on this side, and then on that, and I saw that they in the houses were more comfortable than we in the coach. My book also said of this town, "The inhabitants, in general, are substantial livers."—that is. I suppose, they do not live like philosophers: but, as the stage did not stop long enough for us to dine, we had no opportunity to test the truth of this statement. It may have referred, however, to the quantity "of oil they would yield." It further said, "The inhabitants of Sandwich generally manifest a fond and steady adherence to the manners, employments, and modes of living which characterized their fathers"; which made me think that they were, after all, very much like all the rest of the world;—and it added that this was "a resemblance, which, at this day, will constitute no impeachment of either their virtue or taste": which remark proves to me that the writer was one with the rest of them. No people ever lived by cursing their fathers, however great a curse their fathers might have been to them. But it must be confessed that ours was old authority, and probably they have changed all that now.

An old windmill

Our route was along the Bay side, through Barnstable, Yarmouth, Dennis, and Brewster, to Orleans, with a range of low hills on our right, running down the Cape. The weather was not favorable for wayside views, but we made the most of such glimpses of land and water as we could get through the rain. The country was, for the most part, bare, or with only a little scrubby wood left on the hills. We noticed in Yarmouth—and, if I do not mistake, in Dennis—large tracts where pitch-pines were planted four or five years before. They were in rows, as they appeared when we were abreast of them, and, excepting that there were extensive vacant spaces, seemed to be doing remarkably well. This, we were told, was the only use to which such tracts could be profitably put. Every higher eminence had a pole set up on it, with an old storm-coat or sail tied to it, for a signal, that those on the south side of the Cape, for instance, might know when the Boston packets had arrived on the north. It appeared as if this use must absorb the greater part of the old clothes of the Cape, leaving but few rags for the pedlers. The wind-mills on the hills,—large weather-stained octagonal structures,—and the salt-works scattered all along the shore, with their long rows of vats resting on piles driven into the marsh, their low, turtle-like roofs, and their slighter wind-mills, were novel and interesting objects to an inlander. The sand by the road-side was partially covered with bunches of a moss-like plant, *Hudsonia tomentosa*, which a woman in the stage told us was called "poverty-grass," because it grew where nothing else would.

I was struck by the pleasant equality which reigned among the stage company, and their broad and invulnerable good-humor. They were what is called free and easy, and met one another to advantage, as men who had at length learned how to live. They appeared to know each other when they were strangers, they were so simple and downright. They were well met, in an unusual sense, that is, they met as well as they could meet, and did not seem to be troubled with any impediment. They were not afraid nor ashamed of one another, but were contented to make just such a company as the ingredients allowed. It was evident that the same foolish respect was not here claimed for mere wealth and station that is in many parts of New England; yet some of them were the "first people," as they are called, of the various towns through which we passed. Retired sea-captains, in easy circumstances, who talked of farming as sea-captains are wont; an erect, respectable, and trustworthy-looking man, in his wrapper, some of the salt of the earth, who had formerly been the salt of the sea; or a more courtly gentleman, who, per-chance, had been a representative to the General Court in his day; or a broad, red-faced Cape Cod man, who had seen too many storms to be easily irritated; or a fisherman's wife, who had been waiting a week for a coaster to leave Boston, and had at length come by the cars.

A strict regard for truth obliges us to say that the few women whom we saw that day looked exceedingly pinched up. They had prominent chins and noses, having lost all their teeth, and a sharp *W* would represent their profile. They were not so well preserved as their husbands; or perchance they were well preserved as dried specimens. (Their husbands, however, were pickled.) But we respect them not the less for all that; our own dental system is far from perfect.

Still we kept on in the rain, or, if we stopped, it was commonly at a post-office, and we thought that writing letters, and sorting them against our arrival, must be the principal employment of the inhabitants of the Cape this rainy day. The post-office appeared a singularly domestic institution here. Ever and anon the stage stopped before some low shop or dwelling, and a wheelwright or shoemaker appeared in his shirt sleeves and leather apron, with spectacles newly donned, holding up Uncle Sam's bag, as if it were a slice of home-made cake, for the travellers, while he retailed some piece of gossip to the driver, really as indifferent to the presence of the former as if they were so much baggage. In one instance we understood that a woman was the postmistress, and they said that she made the best one on the road; but we suspected that the letters must be subjected to a very close scrutiny there. While we were stopping for this purpose at Dennis, we ventured to put our heads out of the windows, to see where we were going, and saw rising before us, through the mist, singular barren hills, all stricken with poverty-grass, looming up as if they were in the horizon, though they were close to us, and we seemed to have got to the end of the land on that side, notwithstanding that the horses were still headed that way. Indeed, that part of Dennis which we saw was an exceedingly barren and desolate country, of a character which I can find no name for; such a surface, perhaps, as the bottom of the sea made dry land day before yesterday. It was covered with poverty-grass, and there was hardly a tree in sight, but here and there a little weather-stained, one-storied house, with a red roof,—for often the roof was painted, though the rest of the house was not,—standing bleak and cheerless, yet with a broad foundation to the land, where the comfort must have been all inside. Yet we read in the Gazetteer—for we carried that too with us—that, in 1837, one hundred and fifty masters of vessels, belonging to this town, sailed from the various ports of the Union. There must be many more houses in the south part of the town, else we cannot imagine where they all lodge when they are at home, if ever they are there; but the truth is, their houses are floating ones, and their home is on the ocean. There were almost no trees at all in this part of Dennis, nor could I learn that they talked of setting out any. It is true, there was a meeting-house, set round with Lombardy poplars, in a hollow square, the rows fully as straight as the studs of a building, and the corners as square; but, if I do not mistake, every one of them was dead. I could not help thinking that they needed a revival here. Our book said that, in 1795, there was erected in Dennis "an elegant meeting-house, with a steeple." Perhaps this was the one; though whether it had a steeple, or had died down so far from sympathy with the poplars, I do not remember. Another meeting-house in this town was described as a "neat building"; but of the meeting-house in Chatham, a neigh-boring town, for there was then but one, nothing is said, except that it "is in good repair,"—both which remarks, I trust, may be understood as applying to the churches spiritual as well as material. However, "elegant meeting-houses," from that Trinity one on Broadway, to this at Nobscusset, in my estimation, belong to the same category with "beautiful villages." I was never in season to see one. Handsome is that handsome does. What they did for shade here, in warm weather, we did not know, though we read that "fogs are more frequent in Chatham than in any other part of the country; and they serve in summer, instead of trees, to shelter the houses against the heat of the sun. To those who delight in extensive vision,"—is it to be inferred that the inhabitants of Chatham do not?—"they are unpleasant, but they are not found to be unhealthful." Probably, also, the unobstructed sea-breeze answers the purpose of a fan. The historian of Chatham says further, that "in many families there is no difference between the breakfast and supper; cheese, cakes, and pies being as common at the one as at the other." But that leaves us still uncertain whether they were really common at either.

A street in Sandwich

The road, which was quite hilly, here ran near the Bay-shore, having the Bay on one side, and "the rough hill of Scargo," said to be the highest land on the Cape, on the other. Of the wide prospect of the Bay afforded by the summit of this hill, our guide says: "The view has not much of the beautiful in it, but it communicates a strong emotion of the sublime." That is the kind of communication which we love to have made to us. We passed through the village of Suet, in Dennis, on Suet and Quivet Necks, of which it is said, "when compared with Nobscusset,"—we had a misty recollection of having passed through, or near to, the latter,—"it may be denominated a pleasant village; but, in comparison with the village of Sandwich, there is little or no beauty in it." However, we liked Dennis well, better than any town we had seen on the Cape, it was so novel, and, in that stormy day, so sublimely dreary.

Captain John Sears, of Suet, was the first per-son in this country who obtained pure marine salt by solar evaporation alone; though it had long been made in a similar way on the coast of France, and elsewhere. This was in the year 1776, at which time, on account of the war, salt was scarce and dear. The Historical Collections contain an interesting account of his experiments, which we read when we first saw the roofs of the salt-works. Barnstable county is the most favorable locality for these works on our northern coast,—there is so little fresh water here emptying into ocean. Quite recently there were about two millions of dollars invested in this business here. But now the Cape is unable to compete with the importers of salt and the manufacturers of it at the West, and, accordingly, her salt-works are fast going to decay. From making salt, they turn to fishing more than ever. The Gazetteer will uniformly tell you, under the head of each town, how many go a-fishing, and the value of the fish and oil taken, how much salt is made and used, how many are engaged in the coasting trade, how many in manufacturing palm-leaf hats, leather, boots, shoes, and tinware, and then it has done, and leaves you to imagine the more truly domestic manufactures which are nearly the same all the world over.

Late in the afternoon, we rode through Brewster, so named after Elder Brewster, for fear he would be forgotten else. Who has not heard of Elder Brewster? Who knows who he was? This appeared to be the modern-built town of the Cape, the favorite residence of retired sea-captains. It is said that "there are more masters and mates of vessels which sail on foreign voyages belonging to this place than to any other town in the country." There were many of the modern American houses here, such as they turn out at Cambridgeport, standing on the sand; you could almost swear that they had been floated down Charles River, and drifted across the Bay. I call them American, because they are paid for by Americans, and "put up" by American carpenters; but they are little removed from lumber; only Eastern stuff disguised with white paint, the least interesting kind of drift-wood to me. Perhaps we have reason to be proud of our naval architecture, and need not go to the Greeks, or the Goths, or the Italians, for the models of our vessels. Sea-captains do not employ a Cambridgeport carpenter to build their floating houses, and for their houses on shore, if they must copy any, it would be more agreeable to the imagination to see one of their vessels turned bottom upward, in the Numidian fashion. We read that, "at certain seasons, the reflection of the sun upon the windows of the houses in Well-fleet and Truro (across the inner side of the elbow of the Cape) is discernible with the naked eye, at a distance of eighteen miles and upward, on the county road." This we were pleased to imagine, as we had not seen the sun for twenty-four hours.

The old Higgins tavern at Orleans

The same author (the Rev. John Simpkins) said of the inhabitants, a good while ago: "No persons appear to have a greater relish for the social circle and domestic pleasures. They are not in the habit of frequenting taverns, unless on public occasions. I know not of a proper idler or tavern-haunter in the place." This is more than can be said of my townsmen.

At length we stopped for the night at Higgins's tavern, in Orleans, feeling very much as if we were on a sand-bar in the ocean, and not knowing whether we should see land or water ahead when the mist cleared away. We here overtook two Italian boys, who had waded thus far down the Cape through the sand, with their organs on their backs, and were going on to Provincetown. What a hard lot, we thought, if the Provincetown people should shut their doors against them! Whose yard would they go to next? Yet we concluded that they had chosen wisely to come here, where other music than that of the surf must be rare. Thus the great civilizer sends out its emissaries, sooner or later, to every sandy cape and light-house of the New World which the census-taker visits, and summons the savage there to surrender.

## III

## THE PLAINS OF NAUSET

The next morning, Thursday, October 11th, it rained, as hard as ever; but we were determined to proceed on foot, nevertheless. We first made some inquiries with regard to the practicability of walking up the shore on the Atlantic side to Provincetown, whether we should meet with any creeks or marshes to trouble us. Higgins said that there was no obstruction, and that it was not much farther than by the road, but he thought that we should find it very "heavy" walking in the sand; it was bad enough in the road, a horse would sink in up to the fetlocks there. But there was one man at the tavern who had walked it, and he said that we could go very well, though it was sometimes inconvenient and even dangerous walking under the bank, when there was a great tide, with an easterly wind, which caused the sand to cave. For the first four or five miles we followed the road, which here turns to the north on the elbow, —the narrowest part of the Cape,—that we might clear an inlet from the ocean, a part of Nauset Harbor, in Orleans, on our right. We found the travelling good enough for walkers on the sides of the roads, though it was "heavy" for horses in the middle. We walked with our umbrellas behind us, since it blowed hard as well as rained, with driving mists, as the day before, and the wind helped us over the sand at a rapid rate. Everything indicated that we had reached a strange shore. The road was a mere lane, winding over bare swells of bleak and barren-looking land. The houses were few and far between, besides being small and rusty, though they appeared to be kept in good repair, and their dooryards, which were the unfenced Cape, were tidy; or, rather, they looked as if the ground around them was blown clean by the wind. Perhaps the scarcity of wood here, and the consequent absence of the wood-pile and other wooden traps, had something to do with this appearance. They seemed, like mariners ashore, to have sat right down to enjoy the firmness of the land, without studying their postures or habiliments. To them it was merely *terra firma* and *cognita*, not yet *fertilis* and *jucunda*. Every landscape which is dreary enough has a certain beauty to my eyes, and in this instance its permanent qualities were enhanced by the weather. Everything told of the sea, even when we did not see its waste or hear its roar. For birds there were gulls, and for carts in the fields, boats turned bottom upward against the houses, and sometimes the rib of a whale was woven into the fence by the road-side. The trees were, if possible, rarer than the houses, excepting apple-trees, of which there were a few small orchards in the hollows. These were either narrow and high, with flat tops, having lost their side branches, like huge plum-bushes growing in exposed situations, or else dwarfed and branching immediately at the ground, like quince-bushes. They suggested that, under like circumstances, all trees would at last acquire like habits of growth. I afterward saw on the Cape many full-grown apple-trees not higher than a man's head; one whole orchard, indeed, where all the fruit could have been gathered by a man standing on the ground; but you could hardly creep beneath the trees. Some, which the owners told me were twenty years old, were only three and a half feet high, spreading at six inches from the ground five feet each way, and being withal surrounded with boxes of tar to catch the cankerworms, they looked like plants in flower-pots, and as if they might be taken into the house in the winter. In another place, I saw some not much larger than currant-bushes; yet the owner told me that they had borne a barrel and a half of apples that fall. If they had been placed close together, I could have cleared them all at a jump. I measured some near the Highland Light in Truro, which had been taken from the shrubby woods thereabouts when young, and grafted. One, which had been set ten years, was on an average eighteen inches high, and spread nine feet with a flat top. It had borne one bushel of apples two years before. Another, probably twenty years old from the seed, was five feet high, and spread eighteen feet, branching, as usual, at the ground, so that you could not creep under it. This bore a barrel of apples two years before. The owner of these trees invariably used the personal pronoun in speaking of them; as, "I got *him* out of the woods, but *he* doesn't bear." The largest that I saw in that neighborhood was nine feet high to the topmost leaf, and spread thirty-three feet, branching at the ground five ways.

A Nauset lane

In one yard I observed a single, very healthy-looking tree, while all the rest were dead or dying. The occupant said that his father had manured all but that one with blackfish.

This habit of growth should, no doubt, be encouraged; and they should not be trimmed up, as some travelling practitioners have advised. In 1802 there was not a single fruit-tree in Chatham, the next town to Orleans, on the south; and the old account of Orleans says: "Fruit-trees cannot be made to grow within a mile of the ocean. Even those which are placed at a greater distance are injured by the east winds; and, after violent storms in the spring, a saltish taste is perceptible on their bark." We noticed that they were often covered with a yellow lichen-like rust, the *Parmelia parietina*.

The most foreign and picturesque structures on the Cape, to an inlander, not excepting the salt-works, are the wind-mills,—gray-looking octagonal towers, with long timbers slanting to the ground in the rear, and there resting on a cart-wheel, by which their fans are turned round to face the wind. These appeared also to serve in some measure for props against its force. A great circular rut was worn around the building by the wheel. The neighbors who assemble to turn the mill to the wind are likely to know which way it blows, without a weathercock. They looked loose and slightly locomotive, like huge wounded birds, trailing a wing or a leg, and re-minded one of pictures of the Netherlands. Being on elevated ground, and high in themselves, they serve as landmarks,—for there are no tall trees, or other objects commonly, which can be seen at a distance in the horizon; though the outline of the land itself is so firm and distinct that an insignificant cone, or even precipice of sand, is visible at a great distance from over the sea. Sailors making the land commonly steer either by the wind-mills or the meeting-houses. In the country, we are obliged to steer by the meeting-houses alone. Yet the meeting-house is a kind of wind-mill, which runs one day in seven, turned either by the winds of doctrine or public opinion, or more rarely by the winds of Heaven, where another sort of grist is ground, of which, if it be not all bran or musty, if it be not *plaster*, we trust to make bread of life.

There were, here and there, heaps of shells in the fields, where clams had been opened for bait; for Orleans is famous for its shell-fish, especially clams, or, as our author says, "to speak more properly, worms." The shores are more fertile than the dry land. The inhabitants measure their crops, not only by bushels of corn, but by barrels of clams. A thousand barrels of clam-bait are counted as equal in value to six or eight thousand bushels of Indian corn, and once they were procured without more labor or expense, and the supply was thought to be inexhaustible. "For," runs the history, "after a portion of the shore has been dug over, and almost all the clams taken up, at the end of two years, it is said, they are as plenty there as ever. It is even affirmed by many persons, that it is as necessary to stir the clam ground frequently as it is to hoe a field of potatoes; because, if this labor is omitted, the clams will be crowded too closely together, and will be prevented from increasing in size." But we were told that the small clam, *Mya arenaria*, was not so plenty here as formerly. Probably the clam ground has been stirred too frequently, after all. Nevertheless, one man, who complained that they fed pigs with them and so made them scarce, told me that he dug and opened one hundred and twenty-six dollars' worth in one winter, in Truro.

Nauset Bay

We crossed a brook, not more than fourteen rods long, between Orleans and Eastham, called Jeremiah's Gutter. The Atlantic is said sometimes to meet the Bay here, and isolate the northern part of the Cape. The streams of the Cape are necessarily formed on a minute scale, since there is no room for them to run, without tumbling immediately into the sea; and beside, we found it difficult to run ourselves in that sand, when there was no want of room. Hence, the least channel where water runs, or may run, is important, and is dignified with a name. We read that there is no running water in Chatham, which is the next town. The barren aspect of the land would hardly be believed if described. It was such soil, or rather land, as, to judge from appearances, no farmer in the interior would think of cultivating, or even fencing. Generally, the ploughed fields of the Cape look white and yellow, like a mixture of salt and Indian meal. This is called soil. All an inlander's notions of soil and fertility will be confounded by a visit to these parts, and he will not be able, for some time afterward, to distinguish soil from sand. The historian of Chatham says of a part of that town, which has been gained from the sea: "There is a doubtful appearance of a soil beginning to be formed. It is styled *doubtful,* because it would not be observed by every eye, and perhaps not acknowledged by many." We thought that this would not be a bad description of the greater part of the Cape. There is a "beach" on the west side of Eastham, which we crossed the next summer, half a mile wide, and stretching across the township, containing seventeen hundred acres, on which there is not now a particle of vegetable mould, though it formerly produced wheat. All sands are here called "beaches," whether they are waves of water or of air that dash against them, since they commonly have their origin on the shore. "The sand in some places," says the historian of Eastham, "lodging against the beach-grass, has been raised into hills fifty feet high, where twenty-five years ago no hills existed. In others it has filled up small valleys, and swamps. Where a strong-rooted bush stood, the appearance is singular: a mass of earth and sand adheres to it, resembling a small tower. In several places, rocks, which were formerly covered with soil, are disclosed, and being lashed by the sand, driven against them by the wind, look as if they were recently dug from a quarry."

We were surprised to hear of the great crops of corn which are still raised in Eastham, notwithstanding the real and apparent barrenness. Our landlord in Orleans had told us that he raised three or four hundred bushels of corn annually, and also of the great number of pigs which he fattened. In Champlain's "Voyages," there is a plate representing the Indian cornfields hereabouts, with their wigwams in the midst, as they appeared in 1605, and it was here that the Pilgrims, to quote their own words, "bought eight or ten hogsheads of corn and beans" of the Nauset Indians, in 1622, to keep themselves from starving.[1]

"In 1667 the town [of Eastham] voted that every housekeeper should kill twelve blackbirds or three crows, which did great damage to the corn; and this vote was repeated for many years." In 1695 an additional order was passed, namely, that "every unmarried man in the township shall kill six blackbirds, or three crows, while he remains single; as a penalty for not doing it, shall not be married until he obey this order." The blackbirds, however, still molest the corn. I saw them at it the next summer, and there were many scarecrows, if not scare-blackbirds, in the fields, which I often mistook for men.

A scarecrow

From which I concluded that either many men were not married, or many blackbirds were. Yet they put but three or four kernels in a hill, and let fewer plants remain than we do. In the account of Eastham, in the "Historical Collections," printed in 1802, it is said, that "more corn is produced than the inhabitants consume, and about a thousand bushels are annually sent to market. The soil being free from stones, a plough passes through it speedily; and after the corn has come up, a small Cape horse, somewhat larger than a goat, will, with the assistance of two boys, easily hoe three or four acres in a day; several farmers are accustomed to produce five hundred bushels of grain annually, and not long since one raised eight hundred bushels on sixty acres." Similar accounts are given to-day; indeed, the recent accounts are in some instances suspectable repetitions of the old, and I have no doubt that their statements are as often founded on the exception as the rule, and that by far the greater number of acres are as barren as they appear to be. It is sufficiently remarkable that any crops can be raised here, and it may be owing, as others have suggested, to the amount of moisture in the atmosphere, the warmth of the sand, and the rareness of frosts. A miller, who was sharpening his stones, told me that, forty years ago, he had been to a husking here, where five hundred bushels were husked in one evening, and the corn was piled six feet high or more, in the midst, but now, fifteen or eighteen bushels to an acre were an average yield. I never saw fields of such puny and unpromising looking corn as in this town. Probably the inhabitants are contented with small crops from a great surface easily cultivated. It is not always the most fertile land that is the most profitable, and this sand may repay cultivation, as well as the fertile bottoms of the West. It is said, moreover, that the vegetables raised in the sand, without manure, are remarkably sweet, the pumpkins especially, though when their seed is planted in the interior they soon degenerate. I can testify that the vegetables here, when they succeed at all, look remarkably green and healthy, though perhaps it is partly by contrast with the sand. Yet the inhabitants of the Cape towns, generally, do not raise their own meal or pork. Their gardens are commonly little patches, that have been redeemed from the edges of the marshes and swamps.

All the morning we had heard the sea roar on the eastern shore, which was several miles distant; for it still felt the effects of the storm in which the *St. John* was wrecked,—though a school-boy, whom we overtook, hardly knew what we meant, his ears were so used to it. He would have more plainly heard the same sound in a shell. It was a very inspiriting sound to walk by, filling the whole air, that of the sea dashing against the land, heard several miles inland. Instead of having a dog to growl before your door, to have an Atlantic Ocean to growl for a whole Cape! On the whole, we were glad of the storm, which would show us the ocean in its angriest mood. Charles Darwin was assured that the roar of the surf on the coast of Chiloe, after a heavy gale, could be heard at night a distance of "21 sea miles across a hilly and wooded country." We conversed with the boy we have mentioned, who might have been eight years old, making him walk the while under the lee of our umbrella; for we thought it as important to know what was life on the Cape to a boy as to a man. We learned from him where the best grapes were to be found in that neighborhood. He was carrying his dinner in a pail; and, without any impertinent questions being put by us, it did at length appear of what it consisted. The homeliest facts are always the most acceptable to an inquiring mind. At length, before we got to Eastham meeting-house, we left the road and struck across the country for the eastern shore at Nauset Lights,—three lights close together, two or three miles distant from us. They were so many that they might be distinguished from others; but this seemed a shiftless and costly way of accomplishing that object. We found ourselves at once on an apparently boundless plain, without a tree or a fence, or, with one or two exceptions, a house in sight. Instead of fences, the earth was sometimes thrown up into a slight ridge. My companion compared it to the rolling prairies of Illinois. In the storm of wind and rain which raged when we traversed it, it no doubt appeared more vast and desolate than it really is. As there were no hills, but only here and there a dry hollow in the midst of the waste, and the distant horizon was concealed by mist, we did not know whether it was high or low. A solitary traveller whom we saw perambulating in the distance loomed like a giant. He appeared to walk slouchingly, as if held up from above by straps under his shoulders, as much as supported by the plain below. Men and boys would have appeared alike at a little distance, there being no object by which to measure them. Indeed, to an inlander, the Cape landscape is a constant mirage. This kind of country extended a mile or two each way. These were the "Plains of Nauset," once covered with wood, where in winter the winds howl and the snow blows right merrily in the face of the traveller. I was glad to have got out of the towns, where I am wont to feel unspeakably mean and disgraced,—to have left behind me for a season the bar-rooms of Massachusetts, where the full-grown are not weaned from savage and filthy habits,—still sucking a cigar. My spirits rose in proportion to the outward dreariness. The towns need to be ventilated. The gods would be pleased to see some pure flames from their altars. They are not to be appeased with cigar-smoke.

As we thus skirted the back-side of the towns, for we did not enter any village, till we got to Provincetown, we read their histories under our umbrellas, rarely meeting anybody. The old accounts are the richest in topography, which was what we wanted most; and, indeed, in most things else, for I find that the readable parts of the modern accounts of these towns consist, in a great measure, of quotations, acknowledged and unacknowledged, from the older ones, without any additional information of equal interest;—town histories, which at length run into a history of the Church of that place, that being the only story they have to tell, and conclude by quoting the Latin epitaphs of the old pastors, having been written in the good old days of Latin and of Greek. They will go back to the ordination of every minister and tell you faithfully who made the introductory prayer, and who delivered the sermon; who made the ordaining prayer, and who gave the charge; who extended the right hand of fellowship, and who pronounced the benediction; also how many ecclesiastical councils convened from time to time to inquire into the orthodoxy of some minister, and the names of all who composed them. As it will take us an hour to get over this plain, and there is no variety in the prospect, peculiar as it is, I will read a little in the history of Eastham the while.

When the committee from Plymouth had purchased the territory of Eastham of the Indians, "it was demanded, who laid claim to Billingsgate?" which was understood to be all that part of the Cape north of what they had purchased. "The answer was, there was not any who owned it. 'Then,' said the committee, 'that land is ours.' The Indians answered, that it was." This was a remarkable assertion and admission. The Pilgrims appear to have regarded themselves as Not Any's representatives. Perhaps this was the first instance of that quiet way of "speaking for" a place not yet occupied, or at least not improved as much as it may be, which their descendants have practised, and are still practising so extensively. Not Any seems to have been the sole proprietor of all America before the Yankees. But history says that, when the Pilgrims had held the lands of Billingsgate many years, at length "appeared an Indian, who styled himself Lieutenant Anthony," who laid claim to them, and of him they bought them. Who knows but a Lieutenant Anthony may be knocking at the door of the White House some day? At any rate, I know that if you hold a thing unjustly, there will surely be the devil to pay at last.

Thomas Prince, who was several times the governor of the Plymouth colony, was the leader of the settlement of Eastham. There was recently standing, on what was once his farm, in this town, a pear-tree which is said to have been brought from England, and planted there by him, about two hundred years ago. It was blown down a few months before we were there. A late account says that it was recently in a vigorous state; the fruit small, but excellent; and it yielded on an average fifteen bushels. Some appropriate lines have been addressed to it, by a Mr. Heman Doane, from which I will quote, partly because they are the only specimen of Cape Cod verse which I remember to have seen, and partly because they are not bad.

> "Two hundred years have, on the wings of Time,
>   Passed with their joys and woes, since thou, Old Tree!
> Put forth thy first leaves in this foreign clime.
>   Transplanted from the soil beyond the sea."

\* \* \* \* \*

[These stars represent the more clerical lines, and also those which have deceased.]

> "That exiled band long since have passed away,
>   And still, Old Tree I thou standest in the place
> Where Prince's hand did plant thee in his day,—
>   An undesigned memorial of his race
> And time; of those out honored fathers,
>   when They came from Plymouth o'er and settled here;

>     Doane, Higgins, Snow, and other worthy men.
>     Whose names their sons remember to revere.

* * * * *

> "Old Time has thinned thy boughs. Old Pilgrim Tree!
>     And bowed thee with the weight of many years;
>     Yet 'mid the frosts of age, thy bloom we see,
>     And yearly still thy mellow fruit appears."

There are some other lines which I might quote, if they were not tied to unworthy companions by the rhyme. When one ox will lie down, the yoke bears hard on him that stands up.

One of the first settlers of Eastham was Deacon John Doane, who died in 1707, aged one hundred and ten. Tradition says that he was rocked in a cradle several of his last years. That, certainly, was not an Achillean life. His mother must have let him slip when she dipped him into the liquor which was to make him invulnerable, and he went in, heels and all. Some of the stone-bounds to his farm which he set up are standing to-day, with his initials cut in them.

The ecclesiastical history of this town interested us somewhat. It appears that "they very early built a small meeting-house, twenty feet square, with a thatched roof through which they might fire their muskets,"—of course, at the Devil. "In 1662, the town agreed that a part of every whale cast on shore be appropriated for the support of the ministry." No doubt there seemed to be some propriety in thus leaving the support of the ministers to Providence, whose servants they are, and who alone rules the storms; for, when few whales were cast up, they might suspect that their worship was not acceptable. The ministers must have sat upon the cliffs in every storm, and watched the shore with anxiety. And, for my part, if I were a minister I would rather trust to the bowels of the billows, on the back-side of Cape Cod, to cast up a whale for me, than to the generosity of many a country parish that I know. You cannot say of a country minister's salary, commonly, that it is "very like a whale." Nevertheless, the minister who depended on whales cast up must have had a trying time of it. I would rather have gone to the Falkland Isles with a harpoon, and done with it. Think of a w hale having the breath of life beaten out of him by a storm, and dragging in over the bars and guzzles, for the support of the ministry! What a consolation it must have been to him! I have heard of a minister, who had been a fisherman, being settled in Bridgewater for as long a time as he could tell a cod from a haddock. Generous as it seems, this condition would empty most country pulpits forthwith, for it is long since the fishers of men were fishermen. Also, a duty was put on mackerel here to support a free-school; in other words, the mackerel-school was taxed in order that the children's school might be free. "In 1665 the Court passed a law to inflict corporal punishment on all persons, who resided in the towns of this government, who denied the Scriptures." Think of a man being whipped on a spring morning till he was constrained to confess that the Scriptures were true! "It was also voted by the town that all persons who should stand out of the meeting-house during the time of divine service should be set in the stocks." It behooved such a town to see that sitting in the meeting-house was nothing akin to sitting in the stocks, lest the penalty of obedience to the law might be greater than that of disobedience. This was the Eastham famous of late years for its camp-meetings, held in a grove near by, to which thousands flock from all parts of the Bay. We conjectured that the reason for the perhaps unusual, if not unhealthful, development of the religious sentiment here was the fact that a large portion of the population are women whose husbands and sons are either abroad on the sea, or else drowned, and there is nobody but they and the ministers left behind. The old account says that "hysteric fits are very common in Orleans, Eastham, and the towns below, particularly on Sunday, in the times of divine service. When one woman is affected, five or six others generally sympathize with her; and the congregation is thrown into the utmost confusion. Several old men suppose, unphilosophically and uncharitably, perhaps, that the will is partly concerned, and that ridicule and threats would have a tendency to prevent the evil." How this is now we did not learn. We saw one singularly masculine woman, however, in a house on this very plain, who did not look as if she was ever troubled with hysterics, or sympathized with those that were; or, perchance, life itself was to her a hysteric fit,—a Nauset woman, of a hardness and coarseness such as no man ever possesses or suggests. It was enough to see the vertebrae and sinews of her neck, and her set jaws of iron, which would have bitten a board-nail in two in their ordinary action,—braced against the world, talking like a man-of-war's-man in petticoats, or as if shouting to you through a breaker; who looked as if it made her head ache to live; hard enough for any enormity. I looked upon her as one who had committed infanticide; who never had a brother, unless it were some wee thins: that died in infancy,—for what need of him?—and whose father must have died before she was born. This woman told us that the camp-meetings were not held the previous summer for fear of introducing the cholera, and that they would have been held earlier this summer, but the rye was so backward that straw would not have been re adv for them; for they He in straw. There are sometimes one hundred and fifty ministers (!) and five thousand hearers assembled. The ground, which is called Millennium Grove, is owned by a company in Boston, and is the most suitable, or rather unsuitable, for this purpose of any that I saw on the Cape. It is fenced, and the frames of the tents are at all times to be seen interspersed among the oaks. They have an oven and a pump, and keep all their kitchen utensils and tent coverings and furniture in a permanent building on the spot. They select a time for their meetings when the moon is full. A man is appointed to clear out the pump a week beforehand, while the ministers are clearing their throats; but, probably, the latter do not always deliver as pure a stream as the former. I saw the heaps of clam-shells left under the tables, where they had feasted in previous summers, and supposed, of course, that that was the work of the unconverted, or the backsliders and scoffers. It looked as if a camp-meeting must be a singular combination of a prayer-meeting and a picnic.

Millennium Grove camp-meeting grounds

The first minister settled here was the Rev. Samuel Treat, in 1672, a gentleman who is said to be "entitled to a distinguished rank among the evangelists of New England." He converted many Indians, as well as white men, in his day, and translated the Confession of Faith into the Nauset language. These were the Indians concerning whom their first teacher, Richard Bourne, wrote to Gookin, in 1674, that he had been to see one who was sick, "and there came from him very savory and heavenly expressions," but, with regard to the mass of them, he says, "the truth is, that many of them are very loose in their course, to my heartbreaking sorrow." Mr. Treat is described as a Calvinist of the strictest kind, not one of those who, by giving up or explaining away, become like a porcupine disarmed of its quills, but a consistent Calvinist, who can dart his quills to a distance and courageously defend himself. There exists a volume of his sermons in manuscript, "which," says a commentator, "appear to have been designed for publication." I quote the following sentences at second hand, from a Discourse on Luke xvi. 23, addressed to sinners:—

"Thou must erelong go to the bottomless pit. Hell hath enlarged herself, and is ready to receive thee. There is room enough for thy entertainment....

"Consider, thou art going to a place prepared by God on purpose to exalt his justice in,—a place made for no other employment but torments. Hell is God's house of correction; and, remember, God doth all things like himself. When God would show his justice, and what is the weight of his wrath, he makes a hell where it shall, indeed, appear to purpose.... Woe to thy soul when thou shalt be set up as a butt for the arrows of the Almighty....

"Consider, God himself shall be the principal agent in thy misery,— his breath is the bellows which blows up the flame of hell forever;— and if he punish thee, if he meet thee in his fury, he will not meet thee as a man; he will give thee an omnipotent blow."

"Some think sinning ends with this life; but it is a mistake. The creature is held under an everlasting law; the damned increase in sin in hell. Possibly, the mention of this may please thee. But, remember, there shall be no pleasant sins there; no eating, drinking, singing, dancing, wanton dalliance, and drinking stolen waters, but damned sins, bitter, hellish sins; sins exasperated by torments, cursing God, spite, rage, and blasphemy.—The guilt of all thy sins shall be laid upon thy soul, and be made so many heaps of fuel....

"Sinner, I beseech thee, realize the truth of these things. Do not go about to dream that this is derogatory to God's mercy, and nothing but a vain fable to scare children out of their wits withal. God can be merciful, though he make thee miserable. He shall have monuments enough of that precious attribute, shining like stars in the place of glory, and singing eternal hallelujahs to the praise of Him that redeemed them, though, to exalt the power of his justice, he damn sinners heaps upon heaps."

"But," continues the same writer, "with the advantage of proclaiming the doctrine of terror, which is naturally productive of a sublime and impressive style of eloquence ('Triumphat ventoso gloriæ curru orator, qui pectus angit, irritat, et implet terroribus.' Vid. Burnet,

De Stat. Mort., p. 309), he could not attain the character of a popular preacher. His voice was so loud that it could be heard at a great distance from the meeting-house, even amidst the shrieks of hysterical women, and the winds that howled over the plains of Nauset; but there was no more music in it than in the discordant sounds with which it was mingled."

"The effect of such preaching," it is said, "was that his hearers were several times, in the course of his ministry, awakened and alarmed; and on one occasion a comparatively innocent young man was frightened nearly out of his wits, and Mr. Treat had to exert himself to make hell seem somewhat cooler to him"; yet we are assured that "Treat's manners were cheerful, his conversation pleasant, and sometimes facetious, but always decent. He was fond of a stroke of humor, and a practical joke, and manifested his relish for them by long and loud fits of laughter."

This was the man of whom a well-known anecdote is told, which doubtless many of my readers have heard, but which, nevertheless, I will venture to quote:—

"After his marriage with the daughter of Mr. Willard (pastor of the South Church in Boston), he was sometimes invited by that gentleman to preach in his pulpit. Mr. Willard possessed a graceful delivery, a masculine and harmonious voice; and, though he did not gain much reputation by his 'Body of Divinity,' which is frequently sneered at, particularly by those who have read it, yet in his sermons are strength of thought and energy of language. The natural consequence was that he was generally admired. Mr. Treat having preached one of his best discourses to the congregation of his father-in-law, in his usual unhappy manner, excited universal disgust; and several nice judges waited on Mr. Willard, and begged that Mr. Treat, who was a worthy, pious man, it was true, but a wretched preacher, might never be invited into his pulpit again. To this request Mr. Willard made no reply; but he desired his son-in-law to lend him the discourse; which being left with him, he delivered it without alteration to his people a few weeks after. They ran to Mr. Willard and requested a copy for the press. 'See the difference,' they cried, 'between yourself and your son-in-law; you have preached a sermon on the same text as Mr. Treat's, but whilst his was contemptible, yours is excellent.' As is observed in a note, 'Mr. Willard, after producing the sermon in the handwriting of Mr. Treat, might have addressed these sage critics in the words of Phaedrus,

"'En hic declarat, quales sitis judices.'"[2]

Mr. Treat died of a stroke of the palsy, just after the memorable storm known as the Great Snow, which left the ground around his house entirely bare, but heaped up the snow in the road to an uncommon height. Through this an arched way was dug, by which the Indians bore his bod to the grave.

The reader will imagine us, all the while, steadily traversing that extensive plain in a direction a little north of east toward Nauset Beach, and reading under our umbrellas as we sailed, while it blowed hard with mingled mist and rain, as if we were approaching a fit anniversary of Mr. Treat's funeral. We fancied that it was such a moor as that on which somebody perished in the snow, as is related in the "Lights and Shadows of Scottish Life."

The next minister settled here was the "Rev. Samuel Osborn, who was born in Ireland, and educated at the University of Dublin." He is said to have been "A man of wisdom and virtue," and taught his people the use of peat, and the art of drying and preparing it, which as they had scarcely any other fuel, was a great blessing to them. He also introduced improvements in agriculture. But, notwithstanding his many services, as he embraced the religion of Arminius, some of his flock became dissatisfied. At length, an ecclesiastical council, consisting of ten ministers, with their churches, sat upon him, and they, naturally enough, spoiled his usefulness. The council convened at the desire of two divine philosophers,—Joseph Doane and Nathaniel Freeman.

In their report they say, "It appears to the council that the Rev. Mr. Osborn hath, in his preaching to this people, said, that what Christ did and suffered doth nothing abate or diminish our obligation to obey the law of God, and that Christ's suffering and obedience were for himself; both parts of which, we think, contain dangerous error."

"Also: 'It hath been said, and doth appear to this council, that the Rev. Mr. Osborn, both in public and in private, asserted that there are no promises in the Bible but what are conditional, which we think, also, to be an error, and do say that there are promises which are absolute and without any condition,—such as the promise of a new heart, and that he will write his law in our hearts.'"

"Also, they say, 'it hath been alleged, and doth appear to us, that Mr. Osborn hath declared, that *obedience* is a considerable *cause* of a person's justification, which, we think, contains very dangerous error.'"

And many the like distinctions they made, such as some of my readers, probably, are more familiar with than I am. So, far in the East, among the Yezidis, or Worshippers of the Devil, so-called, the Chaldaeans, and others, according to the testimony of travellers, you may still hear these remarkable disputations on doctrinal points going on. Osborn was, accordingly, dismissed, and he removed to Boston, where he kept school for many years. But he was fully justified, methinks, by his works in the peat-meadow; one proof of which is, that he lived to be between ninety and one hundred years old.

The next minister was the Rev. Benjamin Webb, of whom, though a neighboring clergy-man pronounced him "the best man and the best minister whom he ever knew," yet the historian says that,

"As he spent his days in the uniform discharge of his duty (it reminds one of a country muster) and there were no shades to give relief to his character, not much can be said of him. (Pity the Devil did not plant a few shade-trees along his avenues.) His heart was as pure as the new-fallen snow, which completely covers every dark spot in a field; his mind was as serene as the sky in a mild evening in June, when the moon shines without a cloud. Name any virtue, and that virtue he practised; name any vice, and that vice he shunned. But if peculiar qualities marked his character, they were his humility, his gentleness, and his love of God. The people had long been taught by a son of thunder (Mr. Treat): in him they were instructed by a son of consolation, who sweetly allured them to virtue by soft persuasion, and by exhibiting the mercy of the Supreme Being; for his thoughts were so much in heaven that they seldom descended to the dismal regions below; and though of the same religious sentiments as Mr. Treat, yet his attention was turned to those glad tidings of great joy which a Saviour came to publish."

We were interested to hear that such a man had trodden the plains of Nauset.

Turning over further in our book, our eyes fell on the name of the Rev. Jonathan Bascom, of Orleans; "Senex emunctæ naris, doctus, et auctor elegantium verborum, facetus, et dulcis festique sermonis." And, again, on that of the Rev. Nathan Stone, of Dennis: "Vir humilis, mitis, blandus, advenarum hospes; (there was need of him there;) suis commodis in terrâ non studens, reconditis thesauris in cœlo." An easy virtue that, there, for methinks no inhabitant of Dennis could be very studious about his earthly commodity, but must regard the bulk of his treasures as in heaven. But probably the most just and pertinent character of all is that which appears to be given to the Rev. Ephraim Briggs, of Chatham, in the language of the later Romans, "*Seip, sepoese, sepoemese, wechekum,*"—which not being interpreted, we know not what it means, though we have no doubt it occurs somewhere in the Scriptures, probably in the Apostle Eliot's Epistle to the Nipmucks.

Let no one think that I do not love the old ministers. They were, probably, the best men of their generation, and they deserve that their biographies should fill the pages of the town histories. If I could but hear the "glad tidings" of which they tell, and which, perchance, they heard, I might write in a worthier strain than this.

There was no better way to make the reader realize how wide and peculiar that plain was, and how long it took to traverse it, than by inserting these extracts in the midst of my narrative.

> [1] They touched after this at a place called Mattachiest, where they got more corn; but their shallop being cast away in a storm, the Governor was obliged to return to Plymouth on foot, fifty miles through the woods. According to Mourt's Relation, "he came safely home, though weary and *surbated,*" that is, foot-sore. (Ital. *sobattere,* Lat. *sub* or

*solea battere*, to bruise the soles of the feet; v. Dic. Not "from *acerbatus*, embittered or aggrieved," as one commentator on this passage supposes.) This word is of very rare occurrence, being applied only to governors and persons of like description, who are in that predicament; though such generally have considerable mileage allowed them, and might save their soles if they cared.

[2] Lib. v. Fab. 5.

# IV

## THE BEACH

At length we reached the seemingly retreating boundary of the plain, and entered what had appeared at a distance an upland marsh, but proved to be dry sand covered with Beach-grass, the Bearberry, Bayberry, Shrub-oaks, and Beach-plum, slightly ascending as we approached the shore; then, crossing over a belt of sand on which nothing grew, though the roar of the sea sounded scarcely louder than before, and we were prepared to go half a mile farther, we suddenly stood on the edge of a bluff overlooking the Atlantic. Far below us was the beach, from half a dozen to a dozen rods in width, with a long line of breakers rushing to the strand. The sea was exceedingly dark and stormy, the sky completely overcast, the clouds still dropping rain, and the wind seemed to blow not so much as the exciting cause, as from sympathy with the already agitated ocean. The waves broke on the bars at some distance from the shore, and curving green or yellow as if over so many unseen dams, ten or twelve feet high, like a thousand waterfalls, rolled in foam to the sand. There was nothing but that savage ocean between us and Europe.

Having got down the bank, and as close to the water as we could, where the sand was the hardest, leaving the Nauset Lights behind us, we began to walk leisurely up the beach, in a northwest direction, towards Provincetown, which was about twenty-five miles distant, still sailing under our umbrellas with a strong aft wind, admiring in silence, as we walked, the great force of the ocean stream,—

$$\pi o \tau \alpha \mu o \hat{\imath} o \ \mu \acute{\epsilon} \gamma \alpha \ \sigma \theta \acute{\epsilon} \nu o \varsigma \ \Omega \varkappa \epsilon \alpha \nu o \hat{\imath} o.$$

The white breakers were rushing to the shore; the foam ran up the sand, and then ran back as far as we could see (and we imagined how much farther along the Atlantic coast, before and behind us), as regularly, to compare great things with small, as the master of a choir beats time with his white wand; and ever and anon a higher wave caused us hastily to deviate from our path, and we looked back on our tracks filled with water and foam. The breakers looked like droves of a thousand wild horses of Neptune, rushing to the shore, with their white manes streaming far behind; and when at length the sun shone for a moment, their manes were rainbow-tinted. Also, the long kelp-weed was tossed up from time to time, like the tails of sea-cows sporting in the brine.

A Cape Cod citizen

There was not a sail in sight, and we saw none that day,—for they had all sought harbors in the late storm, and had not been able to get out again; and the only human beings whom we saw on the beach for several days were one or two wreckers looking for drift-wood, and fragments of wrecked vessels. After an easterly storm in the spring, this beach is sometimes strewn with eastern wood from one end to the other, which, as it belongs to him who saves it, and the Cape is nearly destitute of wood, is a Godsend to the inhabitants. We soon met one of these wreckers,—a regular Cape Cod man, with whom we parleyed, with a bleached and weather-beaten face, within whose wrinkles I distinguished no particular feature. It was like an old sail endowed with life,—a hanging cliff of weather-beaten flesh,—like one of the clay boulders which occurred in that sand-bank. He had on a hat which had seen salt water, and a coat of many pieces and colors, though it was mainly the color of the beach, as if it had been sanded. His variegated back—for his coat had many patches, even between the shoulders—was a rich study to us, when we had passed him and looked round. It might have been dishonorable for him to have so many scars behind, it is true, if he had not had many more and more serious ones in front. He looked as if he sometimes saw a doughnut, but never descended to comfort; too grave to laugh, too tough to cry; as indifferent as a clam,—like a sea-clam with hat on and legs, that was out walking the strand. He may have been one of the Pilgrims,—Peregrine White, at least,—who has kept on the back-side of the Cape, and let the centuries go by. He was looking for wrecks, old logs, water-logged and covered with barnacles, or bits of boards and joists, even chips, which he drew out of the reach of the tide, and stacked up to dry. When the log was too large to carry far, he cut it up where the last wave had left it, or rolling it a few feet appropriated it by sticking two sticks into the ground crosswise above it. Some rotten trunk, which in Maine cumbers the ground, and is, perchance, thrown into the water on purpose, is here thus carefully picked up, split and dried, and husbanded. Before winter the wrecker painfully carries these things up the bank on his shoulders by a long diagonal slanting path made with a hoe in the sand, if there is no hollow at hand. You may see his hooked pike-staff always lying on the bank ready for use. He is the true monarch of the beach, whose "right there is none to dispute," and he is as much identified with it as a beach-bird.

Crantz, in his account of Greenland, quotes Dalagen's relation of the ways and usages of the Greenlanders, and says, "Whoever finds driftwood, or the spoils of a shipwreck on the strand, enjoys it as his own, though, he does not live there. But he must haul it ashore and lay a stone upon it, as a token that some one has taken possession of it, and this stone is the deed of security, for no other Greenlander will offer to meddle with it afterwards." Such is the instinctive law of nations. We have also this account of drift-wood in Crantz: "As he (the Founder of Nature) has denied this frigid rocky region the growth of trees, he has bid the streams of the Ocean to convey to its shores a great deal of wood, which accordingly comes floating thither, part without ice, but the most part along with it, and lodges itself between the islands. Were it not for this, we Europeans should have no wood to burn there, and the poor Greenlanders (who, it is true, do not use wood, but train, for burning) would, however, have no wood to roof their houses, to erect their tents, as also to build their boats, and to shaft their arrows (yet there grew some small but crooked alders, &c.), by which they must procure their maintenance, clothing and train for warmth, light, and cooking. Among this wood are great trees torn up by the roots, which by driving up and down for many years and rubbing on the ice, are quite bare of branches and bark, and corroded with great wood-worms. A small part of this drift-wood are willows, alder and birch trees, which come out of the bays in the south of (*i.e.* Greenland); also large trunks of aspen-trees, which must come from a greater distance; but the greatest part is pine and fir. We find also a good deal of a sort of wood finely veined, with few branches; this I fancy is larch-wood, which likes to decorate the sides of lofty, stony mountains. There is also a solid, reddish wood, of a more agreeable fragrance than the common fir, with visible cross-veins; which I take to be the same species as the beautiful silver-firs, or *zirbel*, that have the smell of cedar, and grow on the high Grison hills, and the Switzers wainscot their rooms with them." The wrecker directed us to a slight depression, called Snow's Hollow, by which we ascended the bank,—

for elsewhere, if not difficult, it was inconvenient to climb it on account of the sliding sand, which filled our shoes.

This sand-bank—the backbone of the Cape—rose directly from the beach to the height of a hundred feet or more above the ocean. It was with singular emotions that we first stood upon it and discovered what a place we had chosen to walk on. On our right, beneath us, was the beach of smooth and gently sloping sand, a dozen rods in width; next, the endless series of white breakers; further still, the light green water over the bar, which runs the whole length of the forearm of the Cape, and beyond this stretched the unwearied and illimitable ocean. On our left, extending back from the very edge of the bank, was a perfect desert of shining sand, from thirty to eighty rods in width, skirted in the distance by small sand-hills fifteen or twenty feet high; between which, however, in some places, the sand penetrated as much farther. Next commenced the region of vegetation—a succession of small hills and valleys covered with shrubbery, now glowing with the brightest imaginable autumnal tints; and beyond this were seen, here and there, the waters of the bay. Here, in Wellfleet, this pure sand plateau, known to sailors as the Table Lands of Eastham, on account of its appearance, as seen from the ocean, and because it once made a part of that town,—full fifty rods in width, and in many places much more, and sometimes full one hundred and fifty feet above the ocean,—stretched away northward from the southern boundary of the town, without a particle of vegetation,—as level almost as a table,—for two and a half or three miles, or as far as the eye could reach; slightly rising towards the ocean, then stooping to the beach, by as steep a slope as sand could lie on, and as regular as a military engineer could desire. It was like the escarped rampart of a stupendous fortress, whose glacis was the beach, and whose champaign the ocean.—From its surface we overlooked the greater part of the Cape. In short, we were traversing a desert, with the view of an autumnal landscape of extraordinary brilliancy, a sort of Promised Land, on the one hand, and the ocean on the other. Yet, though the prospect was so extensive, and the country for the most part destitute of trees, a house was rarely visible,—we never saw one from the beach,—and the solitude was that of the ocean and the desert combined. A thousand men could not have seriously interrupted it, but would have been lost in the vastness of the scenery as their footsteps in the sand.

The whole coast is so free from rocks, that we saw but one or two for more than twenty miles. The sand was soft like the beach, and trying to the eyes when the sun shone. A few piles of drift-wood, which some wreckers had painfully brought up the bank and stacked up there to dry, being the only objects in the desert, looked indefinitely large and distant, even like wigwams, though, when we stood near them, they proved to be insignificant little "jags" of wood.

For sixteen miles, commencing at the Nauset Lights, the bank held its height, though farther north it was not so level as here, but interrupted by slight hollows, and the patches of Beach-grass and Bayberry frequently crept into the sand to its edge. There are some pages entitled "A description of the Eastern Coast of the County of Barnstable," printed in 1802, pointing out the spots on which the Trustees of the Humane Society have erected huts called Charity or Humane Houses, "and other places where shipwrecked seamen may look for shelter." Two thousand copies of this were dispersed, that every vessel which frequented this coast might be provided with one. I have read this Shipwrecked Seaman's Manual with a melancholy kind of interest,—for the sound of the surf, or, you might say, the moaning of the sea, is heard all through it, as if its author were the sole survivor of a shipwreck himself. Of this part of the coast he says: "This highland approaches the ocean with steep and lofty banks, which it is extremely difficult to climb, especially in a storm. In violent tempests, during very high tides, the sea breaks against the foot of them, rendering it then unsafe to walk on the strand which lies between them and the ocean. Should the seaman succeed in his attempt to ascend them, he must forbear to penetrate into the country, as houses are generally so remote that they would escape his research during the night; he must pass on to the valleys by which the banks are intersected. These valleys, which the inhabitants call Hollows, run at right angles with the shore, and in the middle or lowest part of them a road leads from the dwelling-houses to the sea." By the *word* road must not always be understood a visible cart-track.

There were these two roads for us,—an upper and a lower one,—the bank and the beach; both stretching twenty-eight miles northwest, from Nauset Harbor to Race Point, without a single opening into the beach, and with hardly a serious interruption of the desert. If you were to ford the narrow and shallow inlet at Nauset Harbor, where there is not more than eight feet of water on the bar at full sea, you might walk ten or twelve miles farther, which would make a beach forty miles long,—and the bank and beach, on the east side of Nantucket, are but a continuation of these. I was comparatively satisfied. There I had got the Cape under me, as much as if I were riding it bare-backed. It was not as on the map, or seen from the stagecoach; but there I found it all out of doors, huge and real, Cape Cod! as it cannot be represented on a map, color it as you will; the thing itself, than which there is nothing more like it, no truer picture or account; which you cannot go farther and see. I cannot remember what I thought before that it was. They commonly celebrate those beaches only which have a hotel on them, not those which have a Humane house alone. But I wished to see that seashore where man's works are wrecks; to put up at the true Atlantic House, where the ocean is land-lord as well as sea-lord, and comes ashore without a wharf for the landing; where the crumbling land is the only invalid, or at best is but dry land, and that is all you can say of it.

We walked on quite at our leisure, now on the beach, now on the bank,—sitting from time to time on some damp log, maple or yellow birch, which had long followed the seas, but had now at last settled on land; or under the lee of a sandhill, on the bank, that we might gaze steadily on the ocean. The bank was so steep that, where there was no danger of its caving, we sat on its edge, as on a bench. It was difficult for us landsmen to look out over the ocean without imagining land in the horizon; yet the clouds appeared to hang low over it, and rest on the water as they never do on the land, perhaps on account of the great distance to which we saw. The sand was not without advantage, for, though it was "heavy" walking in it, it was soft to the feet; and, notwithstanding that it had been raining nearly two days, when it held up for half an hour, the sides of the sand-hills, which were porous and sliding, afforded a dry seat. All the aspects of this desert are beautiful, whether you behold it in fair weather or foul, or when the sun is just breaking out after a storm, and shining on its moist surface in the distance, it is so white, and pure, and level, and each slight inequality and track is so distinctly revealed; and when your eyes slide off this, they fall on the ocean. In summer the mackerel gulls—which here have their nests among the neighboring sand-hills—pursue the traveller anxiously, now and then diving close to his head with a squeak, and he may see them, like swallows, chase some crow which has been feeding on the beach, almost across the Cape.

Though for some time I have not spoken of the roaring of the breakers, and the ceaseless flux and reflux of the waves, yet they did not for a moment cease to dash and roar, with such a tumult that if you had been there, you could scarcely have heard my voice the while; and they are dashing and roaring this very moment, though it may be with less din and violence, for there the sea never rests. We were wholly absorbed by this spectacle and tumult, and like Chryses, though in a different mood from him, we walked silent along the shore of the resounding sea,

Βῆ δ' ἀκέων παρὰ θῖνα πολυφλοίσβοιο θαλάσσης.[1]

I put in a little Greek now and then, partly because it sounds so much like the ocean,—though I doubt if Homer's *Mediterranean* Sea ever sounded so loud as this.

The attention of those who frequent the camp-meetings at Eastham is said to be divided between the preaching of the Methodists and the preaching of the billows on the back-side of the Cape, for they all stream over here in the course of their stay. I trust that in this case the loudest voice carries it. With what effect may we suppose the ocean to say, "My hearers!" to the multitude on the bank! On that side some John N. Maffit; on this, the Reverend Poluphloisboios Thalassa.

There was but little weed cast up here, and that kelp chiefly, there being scarcely a rock for rockweed to adhere to. Who has not had a vision from some vessel's deck, when he had still his land-legs on, of this great brown apron, drifting half upright, and quite submerged through the green water, clasping a stone or a deep-sea mussel in its unearthly fingers? I have seen it carrying a stone half as large as my head. We sometimes watched a mass of this cable-like weed, as it was tossed up on the crest of a breaker, waiting with interest to see it come in, as if there were some treasure buoyed up by it; but we were always surprised and disappointed at the insignificance of the mass which had attracted us. As we looked out over the water, the smallest objects floating on it appeared indefinitely large, we were so impressed by the vastness of the ocean, and each one bore so large a proportion to the whole ocean, which we saw. We were so often disappointed in the size of such things as came ashore, the ridiculous bits of wood or weed, with which the ocean labored, that we began to doubt whether the Atlantic itself would bear a still closer inspection, and wold not turn out to be a but small pond, if it should come ashore to us. This kelp, oar-weed, tangle, devils-apron, sole-leather, or ribbon-weed,—as various species are called,—appeared to us a singularly marine and fabulous product, a lit invention for Neptune to adorn his car with, or a freak of Proteus. All that is told of the sea has a fabulous sound to an inhabitant of the land, and all its products have a certain fabulous quality, as if they belonged to another planet, from sea-weed to a sailor's yarn, or a fish-story. In this element the animal and vegetable kingdoms meet and are strangely mingled. One species of kelp, according to Bory St. Vincent, has a stem fifteen hundred feet long, and hence is the longest vegetable known, and a brig's crew spent two days to no purpose collecting the trunks of another kind cast ashore on the Falkland Islands, mistaking it for drift-wood. (See Harvey on *Algæ*) This species looked almost edible; at least, I thought that if I were starving I would try it. One sailor told me that the cows ate it. It cut like cheese: for I took the earliest opportunity to sit down and deliberately whittle up a fathom or two of it, that I might become more intimately acquainted with it, see how it cut, and if it were hollow all the way through. The blade looked like a broad belt, whose edges had been quilled, or as if stretched by hammering, and it was also twisted spirally. The extremity was generally worn and ragged from the lashing of the waves. A piece of the stem which I carried home shrunk to one quarter of its size a week afterward, and was completely covered with crystals of salt like frost. The reader will excuse my greenness,—though it is not sea-greenness, like his, perchance,—for I live by a river-shore, where this weed does not wash up. When we consider in what meadows it grew. and how it was raked, and in what kind of hay weather got in or out, we may well be curious about it. One who is weatherwise has given the following account of the matter.

"When descends on the Atlantic
    The gigantic
  Storm-wind of the equinox,
Landward in his wrath he scourges
    The toiling surges,
Laden with sea-weed from the rocks.

"From Bermuda's reefs, from edges
    Of sunken ledges,
  On some far-off bright Azore;
From Bahama and the dashing,
    Silver-flashing
Surges of San Salvador;

"From the trembling surf that buries
    The Orkneyan Skerries.
  Answering the hoarse Hebrides;
And from wrecks and ships and drifting
    Spars, uplifting
On the desolate rainy seas;

"Ever drifting, drifting, drifting
On the shifting
Currents of the restless main."

But he was not thinking of this shore, when he added:—

>    "Till, in sheltered coves and reaches
>       Of sandy beaches,
>    All have found repose again."

*These* weeds were the symbols of those grotesque and fabulous thoughts which have not yet got into the sheltered coves of literature.

>    "Ever drifting, drifting, drifting
>       On the shifting
>    Currents of the restless heart,"
> *And not yet* "in books recorded
>       They, like hoarded
>    Household words, no more depart."

The beach was also strewn with beautiful sea-jellies, which the wreckers called Sun-squall, one of the lowest forms of animal life, some white, some wine-colored, and a foot in diameter. I at first thought that they were a tender part of some marine monster, which the storm or some other foe had mangled. What right has the sea to bear in its bosom such tender things as sea-jellies and mosses, when it has such a boisterous shore that the stoutest fabrics are wrecked against it? Strange that it should undertake to dandle such delicate children in its arm. I did not at first recognize these for the same which I had formerly seen in myriads in Boston Harbor, rising, with a waving motion, to the surface, as if to meet the sun, and discoloring the waters far and wide, so that I seemed to be sailing through a mere sunfish soup. They say that when you endeavor to take one up, it will spill out the other side of your hand like quicksilver. Before the land rose out of the ocean, and became *dry* land, chaos reigned; and between high and low water mark, where she is partially disrobed and rising, a sort of chaos reigns still, which only anomalous creatures can inhabit. Mackerel-gulls were all the while flying over our heads and amid the breakers, sometimes two white ones pursuing a black one; quite at home in the storm, though they are as delicate organizations as sea-jellies and mosses; and we saw that they were adapted to their circumstances rather by their spirits than their bodies. Theirs must be an essentially wilder, that is, less human, nature than that of larks and robins. Their note was like the sound of some vibrating metal, and harmonized well with the scenery and the roar of the surf, as if one had rudely touched the strings of the lyre, which ever lies on the shore; a ragged shred of ocean music tossed aloft on the spray. But if I were required to name a sound the remembrance of which most perfectly revives the impression which the beach has made, it would be the dreary peep of the piping plover (*Charadrius melodus*) which haunts there. Their voices, too, are heard as a fugacious part in the dirge which is ever played along the shore for those mariners who have been lost in the deep since first it was created. But through all this dreariness we seemed to have a pure and unqualified strain of eternal melody, for always the same strain which is a dirge to one household is a morning song of rejoicing to another.

A remarkable method of catching gulls, derived from the Indians, was practised in Wellfleet in 1794. "The Gull House," it is said, "is built with crotchets, fixed in the ground on the beach," poles being stretched across for the top, and the sides made close with stakes and seaweed. "The poles on the top are covered with lean whale. The man being placed within, is not discovered by the fowls, and while they are contending for and eating the flesh, he draws them in, one by one, between the poles, until he has collected forty or fifty." Hence, perchance, a man is said to be *gulled*, when he is *taken in*. We read that one "sort of gulls is called by the Dutch *mallemucke, i.e.* the foolish fly, because they fall upon a whale as eagerly as a fly, and, indeed, all gulls are foolishly bold and easy to be shot. The Norwegians call this bird *havhest*, sea-horse (and the English translator says, it is probably what we call boobies). If they have eaten too much, they throw it up, and eat it again till they are tired. It is this habit in the gulls of parting with their property [disgorging the contents of their stomachs to the skuas], which has given rise to the terms gull, guller, and gulling, among men." We also read that they used to kill small birds which roosted on the beach at night, by making a fire with hog's lard in a frying-pan. The Indians probably used pine torches; the birds flocked to the light, and were knocked down with a stick. We noticed holes dug near the edge of the bank, where gunners conceal themselves to shoot the large gulls which coast up and down a-fishing, for these are considered good to eat.

We found some large clams of the species *Mactra solidissima*, which the storm had torn up from the bottom, and cast ashore. I selected one of the largest, about six inches in length, and carried it along, thinking to try an experiment on it. We soon after met a wrecker, with a grapple and a rope, who said that he was looking for tow cloth, which had made part of the cargo of the ship *Franklin*, which was wrecked here in the spring, at which time nine or ten lives were lost. The reader may remember this wreck, from the circumstance that a letter was found in the captain's valise, which washed ashore, directing him to wreck the vessel before he got to America, and from the trial which took place in consequence. The wrecker said that tow cloth was still cast up in such storms as this. He also told us that the clam which I had was the sea-clam, or hen, and was good to eat. We took our nooning under a sand-hill, covered with beach-grass, in a dreary little hollow, on the top of the bank, while it alternately rained and shined. There, having reduced some damp drift-wood, which I had picked up on the shore, to shavings with my knife, I kindled a fire with a match and some paper and cooked my clam on the embers for my dinner; for breakfast was commonly the only meal which I took in a house on this excursion. When the clam was done, one valve held the meat and the other the liquor. Though it was very tough, I found it sweet and savory, and ate *the whole* with a relish. Indeed, with the addition of a cracker or two, it would have been a bountiful dinner. I noticed that the shells were such as I had seen in the sugar-kit at home. Tied to a stick, they formerly made the Indian's hoe hereabouts.

At length, by mid-afternoon, after we had had two or three rainbows over the sea, the showers ceased, and the heavens gradually cleared up, though the wind still blew as hard and the breakers ran as high as before. Keeping on, we soon after came to a Charity-house, which we looked into to see how the shipwrecked mariner might fare. Far away in some desolate hollow by the sea-side, just within the bank, stands a lonely building on piles driven into the sand, with a slight nail put through the staple, which a freezing man can bend, with some straw, perchance, on the floor on which he may lie, or which he may burn in the fireplace to keep him alive. Perhaps this hut has never been required to shelter a ship-wrecked man, and the benevolent person who promised to inspect it annually, to see that the straw and matches are here, and that the boards will keep off the wind, has grown remiss and thinks that storms and shipwrecks are over; and this very night a perishing crew may pry open its door with their numbed fingers and leave half their number dead here by morning. When I thought what must be the condition of the families which alone would ever occupy or had occupied them, what must have been the tragedy of the winter evenings spent by human beings around their hearths, these houses, though they were meant for human dwellings, did not look cheerful to me. They appeared but a stage to the grave. The gulls flew around and screamed over them; the roar of the ocean in storms, and the lapse of its waves in calms, alone resounds through them, all dark and empty within, year in, year out, except, perchance, on one memorable night. Houses of entertainment for shipwrecked men! What kind of sailors' homes were they?

Wreckage under the sand-bluff

"Each hut," says the author of the "Description of the Eastern Coast of the County of Barnstable," "stands on piles, is eight feet long, eight feet wide, and seven feet high; a sliding door is on the south, a sliding shutter on the west, and a pole, rising fifteen feet above the top of the building, on the east. Within it is supplied either with straw or hay, and is further accommodated with a bench." They have varied little from this model now. There are similar huts at the Isle of Sable and Anticosti, on the north, and how far south along the coast I know not. It is pathetic to read the minute and faithful directions which he gives to seamen who may be wrecked on this coast, to guide them to the nearest Charity-house, or other shelter, for, as is said of Eastham, though there are a few houses within a mile of the shore, yet "in a snow-storm, which rages here with excessive fury, it would be almost impossible to discover them either by night or by day." You hear their imaginary guide thus marshalling, cheering, directing the dripping, shivering, freezing troop along; "at the entrance of this valley the sand has gathered, so that at present a little climbing is necessary. Passing over several fences and taking heed not to enter the wood on the right hand, at the distance of three-quarters of a mile a house is to be found. This house stands on the south side of the road, and not far from it on the south is Pamet River, which runs from east to west through body of salt marsh." To him cast ashore in Eastham, he says, "The meeting-house is without a steeple, but it may be distinguished from the dwelling-houses near it by its situation, which is between two small groves of locusts, one on the south and one on the north,—that on the south being three times as long as the other. About a mile and a quarter from the hut, west by north, appear the top and arms of a windmill." And so on for many pages.

We did not learn whether these houses had been the means of saving any lives, though this writer says, of one erected at the head of Stout's Creek in Truro, that "it was built in an improper manner, having a chimney in it; and was placed on a spot where no beach-grass grew. The strong winds blew the sand from its foundation and the weight of the chimney brought it to the ground; so that in January of the present year [1802] it was entirely demolished. This event took place about six weeks before the *Brutus* was cast away. If it had remained, it is probable that the whole of the unfortunate crew of that ship would have been saved, as they gained the shore a few rods only from the spot where the hut had stood."

This "Charity-house," as the wrecker called it, this "Humane-house," as some call it, that is, the one to which we first came, had neither window nor sliding shutter, nor clapboards, nor paint. As we have said, there was a rusty nail put through the staple. However, as we wished to get an idea of a Humane house, and we hoped that we should never have a better opportunity, we put our eyes, by turns, to a knot-hole in the door, and after long looking, without seeing, into the dark,—not knowing how many shipwrecked men's bones we might see at last, looking with the eye of faith, knowing that, though to him that knocketh it may not always be opened, yet to him that looketh long enough through a knot-hole the inside shall be visible,—for we had had some practice at looking inward,—by steadily keeping our other ball covered from the light meanwhile, putting the outward world behind us, ocean and land, and the beach,—till the pupil became enlarged and collected the rays of light that were wandering in that dark (for the pupil shall be enlarged by looking; there never was so dark a night but a faithful and patient eye, however small, might at last prevail over it),—after all this, I say, things began to take shape to our vision,—if we may use this expression where there was nothing but emptiness,—and we obtained the long-wished-for insight. Though we thought at first that it was a hopeless case, after several minutes' steady exercise of the divine faculty, our prospects began decidedly to brighten, and we were ready to exclaim with the blind bard of "Paradise Lost and Regained,"—

"Hail, holy Light! offspring of Heaven first born,

Or of the Eternal co-eternal beam.

May I express thee unblamed?"

A little longer, and a chimney rushed red on our sight. In short, when our vision had grown familiar with the darkness, we discovered that there were some stones and some loose wads of wool on the floor, and an empty fireplace at the further end; but it *was not* supplied with matches, or straw, or hay, that we could see, nor "accommodated with a bench." Indeed, it was the wreck of all cosmical beauty there within.

Turning our backs on the outward world, we thus looked through the knot-hole into the Humane house, into the very bowels of mercy; and for bread we found a stone. It was literally a great cry (of sea-mews outside), and a little wool. However, we were glad to sit outside, under the lee of the Humane house, to escape the piercing wind; and there we thought how cold is charity! how inhumane humanity! This, then, is what charity hides! Virtues antique and far away with ever a rusty nail over the latch; and very difficult to keep in repair, withal, it is so uncertain whether any will ever gain the beach near you. So we shivered round about, not being able to get into it, ever and anon looking through the knot-hole into that night without a star, until we concluded that it was not a *humane* house at all, but a sea-side box, now shut up. belonging to some of the family of Night or Chaos, where they spent their summers by the sea, for the sake of the sea breeze, and that it was not proper for us to be prying into their concerns.

My companion had declared before this that I had not a particle of sentiment, in rather absolute terms, to my astonishment; but I suspect he meant that my legs did not ache just then, though I am not wholly a stranger to that sentiment. But I did not intend this for a sentimental journey.

Herring River at Wellfleet

[1] We have no word in English to express the sound of many waves, dashing at once, whether gently or violently, πολυφλοίσβοιος to the ear, and, in the ocean's gentle moods, an ἀνάριθμον γέλασμα to the eye.

## V

## THE WELLFLEET OYSTERMAN

Having walked about eight miles since we struck the beach, and passed the boundary between Wellfleet and Truro, a stone post in the sand,—for even this sand comes under the jurisdiction of one town or another,—we turned inland over barren hills and valleys, whither the sea, for some reason, did not follow us, and, tracing up a Hollow, discovered two or three sober-looking houses within half a mile, uncommonly near the eastern coast. Their garrets were apparently so full of chambers, that their roofs could hardly lie down straight, and we did not doubt that there was room for us there. Houses near the sea are generally low and broad. These were a story and a half high; but if you merely counted the windows in their gable-ends, you would think that there were many stories more, or, at any rate, that the half-story was the only one thought worthy of being illustrated. The great number of windows in the ends of the houses, and their irregularity in size and position, here and elsewhere on the Cape, struck us agreeably,—as if each of the various occupants who had their *cunabula* behind had punched a hole where his necessities required it, and, according to his size and stature, without regard to outside effect. There were windows for the grown folks, and windows for the children,—three or four apiece; as a certain man had a large hole cut in his barn-door for the cat, and another smaller one for the kitten. Sometimes they were so low under the eaves that I thought they must have perforated the plate beam for another apartment, and I noticed some which were triangular, to fit that part more exactly. The ends of the houses had thus as many muzzles as a revolver, and, if the inhabitants have the same habit of staring out the windows that some of our neighbors have, a traveller must stand a small chance with them.

Generally, the old-fashioned and unpainted houses on the Cape looked more comfortable, as well as picturesque, than the modern and more pretending ones, which were less in harmony with the scenery, and less firmly planted.

A characteristic gable with many windows

These houses were on the shores of a chain of ponds, seven in number, the source of a small stream called Herring River, which empties into the Bay. There are many Herring Rivers on the Cape; they will, perhaps, be more numerous than herrings soon. We knocked at the door of the first house, but its inhabitants were all gone away. In the meanwhile, we saw the occupants of the next one looking out the window at us, and before we reached it an old woman came out and fastened the door of her bulkhead, and went in again. Nevertheless, we did not hesitate to knock at her door, when a grizzly-looking man appeared, whom we took to be sixty or seventy years old. He asked us, at first, suspiciously, where we were from, and what our business was; to which we returned plain answers.

"How far is Concord from Boston?" he inquired.

"Twenty miles by railroad."

"Twenty miles by railroad," he repeated.

"Didn't you ever hear of Concord of Revolutionary fame?"

"Didn't I ever hear of Concord? Why, I heard the guns fire at the battle of Bunker Hill. [They hear the sound of heavy cannon across the Bay.] I am almost ninety; I am eighty-eight year old. I was fourteen year old at the time of Concord Fight,—and where were you then?"

We were obliged to confess that we were not in the fight.

"Well, walk in, we'll leave it to the women," said he.

So we walked in, surprised, and sat down, an old woman taking our hats and bundles, and the old man continued, drawing up to the large, old-fashioned fireplace,—

"I am a poor good-for-nothing crittur, as Isaiah says; I am all broken down this year. I am under petticoat government here."

The family consisted of the old man, his wife, and his daughter, who appeared nearly as old as her mother, a fool, her son (a brutish-looking, middle-aged man, with a prominent lower face, who was standing by the hearth when we entered, but immediately went out), and a little boy of ten.

While my companion talked with the women, I talked with the old man. They said that he was old and foolish, but he was evidently too knowing for them.

"These women," said he to me, "are both of them poor good-for-nothing critturs. This one is my wife. I married her sixty-four years ago. She is eighty-four years old, and as deaf as an adder, and the other is not much better."

He thought well of the Bible, or at least he *spoke* well, and did not *think* ill, of it, for that would not have been prudent for a man of his age. He said that he had read it attentively for many years, and he had much of it at his tongue's end. He seemed deeply impressed with a sense of his own nothingness, and would repeatedly exclaim,—

"I am a nothing. What I gather from my Bible is just this: that man is a poor good-for-nothing crittur, and everything is just as God sees fit and disposes."

"May I ask your name?" I said.

"Yes," he answered, "I am not ashamed to tell my name. My name is——. My great-grandfather came over from England and settled here."

He was an old Wellfleet oysterman, who had acquired a competency in that business, and had sons still engaged in it.

Nearly all the oyster shops and stands in Massachusetts, I am told, are supplied and kept by natives of Wellfleet, and a part of this town is still called Billingsgate from the oysters having been formerly planted there; but the native oysters are said to have died in 1770. Various causes are assigned for this, such as a ground frost, the carcasses of blackfish kept to rot in the harbor, and the like, but the most common account of the matter is,—and I find that a similar superstition with regard to the disappearance of fishes exists almost everywhere,—that when Wellfleet began to quarrel with the neighboring towns about the right to gather them, yellow specks appeared in them, and Providence caused them to disappear. A few years ago sixty thousand bushels were annually brought from the South and planted in the harbor of Wellfleet till they attained "the proper relish of Billingsgate"; but now they are imported commonly full-grown, and laid down near their markets, at Boston and elsewhere, where the water, being a mixture of salt and fresh, suits them better. The business was said to be still good and improving.

The old man said that the oysters were liable to freeze in the winter, if planted too high; but if it were not "so cold as to strain their eyes" they were not injured. The inhabitants of New Brunswick have noticed that "ice will not form over an oyster-bed, unless the cold is very intense indeed, and when the bays are frozen over the oyster-beds are easily discovered by the water above them remaining unfrozen, or as the French residents say, *degèle*." Our host said that they kept them in cellars all winter.

"Without anything to eat or drink?" I asked.

"Without anything to eat or drink," he answered.

"Can the oysters move?"

"Just as much as my shoe."

A Welfleet oysterman

But when I caught him saying that they "bedded themselves down in the sand, flat side up, round side down," I told him that my shoe could not do that, without the aid of my foot in it; at which he said that they merely settled down as they grew; if put down in a square they would be found so; but the clam could move quite fast. I have since been told by oystermen of Long Island, where the oyster is still indigenous and abundant, that they are found in large masses attached to the parent in their midst, and are so taken up with their tongs; in which case, they say, the age of the young proves that there could have been no motion for five or six years at least. And Buckland in his Curiosities of Natural History (page 50) says: "An oyster who has once taken up his position and fixed himself when quite young can never make a change. Oysters, nevertheless, that have not fixed themselves, but remain loose at the bottom of the sea, have the power of locomotion; they open their shells to their fullest extent, and then suddenly contracting them, the expulsion of the water forwards gives a motion backwards. A fisherman at Guernsey told me that he had frequently seen oysters moving in this way."

Some still entertain the question "whether the oyster was indigenous in Massachusetts Bay," and whether Wellfleet harbor was a "natural habitat" of this fish; but, to say nothing of the testimony of old oystermen, which, I think, is quite conclusive, though the native oyster may now be extinct there, I saw that their shells, opened by the Indians, were strewn all over the Cape. Indeed, the Cape was at first thickly settled by Indians on account of the abundance of these and other fish. We saw many traces of their occupancy after this, in Truro, near Great Hollow, and at High-Head, near East Harbor River,— oysters, clams, cockles, and other shells, mingled with ashes and the bones of deer and other quadrupeds. I picked up half a dozen arrowheads, and in an hour or two could have filled my pockets with them. The Indians lived about the edges of the swamps, then probably in some instances ponds, for shelter and water. Moreover, Champlain in the edition of his "Voyages" printed in 1613, says that in the year 1606 he and Poitrincourt explored a harbor (Barnstable Harbor?) in the southerly part of what is now called Massachusetts Bay, in latitude 42°, about five leagues south, one point west of *Cap Blanc* (Cape Cod), and there they found many good oysters, and they named it *"le Port aux Huistres"* (Oyster Harbor). In one edition of his map (1632), the *"R. aux Escailles"* is drawn emptying into the same part of the bay, and on the map *"Novi Belgii,"* in Ogilby's "America" (1670), the words *"Port aux Huistres"* are placed against the same place. Also William Wood, who left New England in 1633, speaks, in his "New England's Prospect," published in 1634, of "a great oyster-bank" in Charles River, and of another in the Mistick, each of which obstructed the navigation of its river. "The oysters," says he, "be great ones in form of a shoehorn; some be a foot long; these breed on certain banks that are bare every spring tide. This fish without the shell is so big, that it must admit of a division before you can well get it into your mouth." Oysters are still found there. (Also, see Thomas Morton's "New English Canaan," page 90.)

Our host told us that the sea-clam, or hen, was not easily obtained; it was raked up, but never on the Atlantic side, only cast ashore there in small quantities in storms. The fisherman sometimes wades in water several feet deep, and thrusts a pointed stick into the sand before him. When this enters between the valves of a clam, he closes them on it, and is drawn out. It has been known to catch and hold coot and teal which were preying on it. I chanced to be on the bank of the Acushnet at New Bedford one day since this, watching some ducks, when a man informed me that, having let out his young ducks to seek their food amid the samphire (*Salicornia*) and other weeds along the river-side at low tide that morning, at length he noticed that one remained stationary, amid the weeds, something preventing it from following the others, and going to it he found its foot tightly shut in a quahog's shell. He took up both together, carried them to his home, and his wife opening the shell with a knife released the duck and cooked the quahog. The old man said that the great clams were good to eat, but that they always took out a certain part which was poisonous, before they cooked them. "People said it would kill a cat." I did not tell him that I had eaten a large one entire that afternoon, but began to think that I was tougher than a cat. He stated that pedlers came round there, and sometimes tried to sell the women folks a skimmer, but he told them that their women had got a better skimmer than *they* could make, in the shell of their clams; it was shaped just right for this purpose.— They call them "skim-alls" in some places. He also said that the sun-squall was poisonous to handle, and when the sailors came across it, they did not meddle with it, but heaved it out of their way. I told him that I had handled it that afternoon, and had felt no ill effects as yet. But he said it made the hands itch, especially if they had previously been scratched, or if I put it into my bosom I should find out what it was.

He informed us that no ice ever formed on the back side of the Cape, or not more than once in a century, and but little snow lay there, it being either absorbed or blown or washed away. Sometimes in winter, when the tide was down, the beach was frozen, and afforded a hard road up the back side for some thirty miles, as smooth as a floor. One winter when he was a boy, he and his father "took right out into the back side before daylight, and walked to Provincetown and back to dinner."

When I asked what they did with all that barren-looking land, where I saw so few cultivated fields,—"Nothing," he said.

"Then why fence your fields?"

"To keep the sand from blowing and covering up the whole."

"The yellow sand," said he, "has some life in it, but the white little or none."

When, in answer to his questions, I told him that I was a surveyor, he said that they who surveyed his farm were accustomed, where the ground was uneven, to loop up each chain as high as their elbows; that was the allowance they made, and he wished to know if I could tell him why they did not come out according to his deed, or twice alike. He seemed to have more respect for surveyors of the old school, which I did not wonder at. "King George the Third," said he, "laid out a road four rods wide and straight the whole length of the Cape," but where it was now he could not tell.

This story of the surveyors reminded me of a Long-Islander, who once, when I had made ready to jump from the bow of his boat to the shore, and he thought that I underrated the distance and would fall short,—though I found afterward that he judged of the elasticity of my joints by his own,—told me that when he came to a brook which he wanted to get over, he held up one leg, and then, if his foot appeared to cover any part of the opposite bank, he knew that he could jump it. "Why," I told him, "to say nothing of the Mississippi, and other small watery streams, I could blot out a star with my foot, but I would not engage to jump that distance," and asked how he knew when he had got his leg at the right elevation. But he regarded his legs as no less accurate than a pair of screw dividers or an ordinary quadrant, and appeared to have a painful recollection of every degree and minute in the arc which they described; and he would have had me believe that there was a kind of hitch in his hip-joint which answered the purpose. I suggested that he should connect his two ankles by a string of the proper length, which should be the chord of an arc, measuring his jumping ability on horizontal surfaces,—assuming one leg to be a perpendicular to the plane of the horizon, which, however, may have been too bold an assumption in this case. Nevertheless, this was a kind of geometry in the legs which it interested me to hear of.

Our host took pleasure in telling us the names of the ponds, most of which we could see from his windows, and making us repeat them after him, to see if we had got them right. They were Gull Pond, the largest and a very handsome one, clear and deep, and more than a mile in circumference, Newcomb's, Swett's, Slough, Horse-Leech, Round, and Herring Ponds, all connected at high water, if I do not mistake. The coast-surveyors had come to him for their names, and he told them of one which they had not detected. He said that they were not so high as formerly. There was an earthquake about four years before he was born, which cracked the pans of the ponds, which were of iron, and caused them to settle. I did not remember to have read of this. Innumerable gulls used to resort to them; but the large gulls were now very scarce, for, as he said, the English robbed their nests far in the north, where they breed. He remembered well when gulls were taken in the gull-house, and when small birds were killed by means of a frying-pan and fire at night. His father once lost a valuable horse from this cause. A party from Wellfleet having lighted their fire for this purpose, one dark night, on Billingsgate Island, twenty horses which were pastured there, and this colt among them, being frightened by it, and endeavoring in the dark to cross the passage which separated them from the neighboring beach, and which was then fordable at low tide, were all swept out to sea and drowned. I ob-served that many horses were still turned out to pasture all summer on the islands and beaches in Wellfleet, Eastham, and Orleans, as a kind of common. He also described the killing of what he called "wild hens" here, after they had gone to roost in the woods, when he was a boy. Perhaps they were "Prairie hens" (pinnated grouse).

He liked the Beach-pea (*Lathyrus maritimus*), cooked green, as well as the cultivated. He had seen it growing very abundantly in Newfoundland, where also the inhabitants ate them, but he had never been able to obtain any ripe for seed. We read, under the head of Chatham, that "in 1555, during a time of great scarcity, the people about Orford, in Sussex (England) were preserved from perishing by eating the seeds of this plant, which grew there in great abundance on the sea-coast. Cows, horses, sheep, and goats eat it." But the writer who quoted this could not learn that they had ever been used in Barnstable County.

He had been a voyager, then? O, he had been about the world in his day. He once considered himself a pilot for all our coast; but now they had changed the names so he might be bothered.

He gave us to taste what he called the Summer Sweeting, a pleasant apple which he raised, and frequently grafted from, but had never seen growing elsewhere, except once,—three trees on Newfoundland, or at the Bay of Chaleur, I forget which, as he was sailing by. He was sure that he could tell the tree at a distance.

At length the fool, whom my companion called the wizard, came in, muttering between his teeth, "Damn book-pedlers,—all the time talking about books. Better do something. Damn 'em. I'll shoot 'em. Got a doctor down here. Damn him, I'll get a gun and shoot him"; never once holding up his head. Whereat the old man stood up and said in a loud voice, as if he was accustomed to command, and this was not the first time he had been obliged to exert his authority there: "John, go sit down, mind your business,—we've heard you talk before,—precious little you'll do,—your bark is worse than your bite." But, without minding, John muttered the same gibberish over again, and then sat down at the table which the old folks had left. He ate all there was on it, and then turned to the apples, which his aged mother was paring, that she might give her guests some apple-sauce for breakfast, but she drew them away and sent him off.

Welfleet

When I approached this house the next summer, over the desolate hills between it and the shore, which are worthy to have been the birthplace of Ossian, I saw the wizard in the midst of a cornfield on the hillside, but, as usual, he loomed so strangely, that I mistook him for a scarecrow.

This was the merriest old man that we had ever seen, and one of the best preserved. His style of conversation was coarse and plain enough to have suited Rabelais. He would have made a good Panurge. Or rather he was a sober Silenus, and we were the boys Chromis and Mnasilus, who listened to his story.

> "Not by Hæmonian hills the Thracian bard.
> Nor awful Phœbus was on Pindus heard
> With deeper silence or with more regard."

There was a strange mingling of past and present in his conversation, for he had lived under King George, and might have remembered when Napoleon and the moderns generally were born. He said that one day, when the troubles between the Colonies and the mother country first broke out, as he, a boy of fifteen, was pitching hay out of a cart, one Doane, an old Tory, who was talking with his father, a good Whig, said to him, "Why, Uncle Bill, you might as well undertake to pitch that pond into the ocean with a pitchfork, as for the Colonies to undertake to gain their independence." He remembered well General Washington, and how he rode his horse along the streets of Boston, and he stood up to show us how he looked.

"He was a r—a—ther large and portly-looking man, a manly and resolute-looking officer, with a pretty good leg as he sat on his horse."—"There, I'll tell you, this was the way with Washington." Then he jumped up again, and bowed gracefully to right and left, making show as if he were waving his hat. Said he, *"That* was Washington."

He told us many anecdotes of the Revolution, and was much pleased when we told him that we had read the same in history, and that his account agreed with the written.

"O," he said, "I know, I know! I was a young fellow of sixteen, with my ears wide open; and a fellow of that age, you know, is pretty wide awake, and likes to know everything that's going on. O, I know!"

He told us the story of the wreck of the *Franklin*, which took place there the previous spring: how a boy came to his house early in the morning to know whose boat that was by the shore, for there was a vessel in distress, and he, being an old man, first ate his breakfast, and then walked over to the top of the hill by the shore, and sat down there, having found a comfortable seat, to see the ship wrecked. She was on the bar, only a quarter of a mile from him, and still nearer to the men on the beach, who had got a boat ready, but could render no assistance on account of the breakers, for there was a pretty high sea running. There were the passengers all crowded together in the forward part of the ship, and some were getting out of the cabin windows and were drawn on deck by the others.

"I saw the captain get out his boat," said he; "he had one little one; and then they jumped into it one after another, down as straight as an arrow. I counted them. There were nine. One was a woman, and she jumped as straight as any of them. Then they shoved off. The sea took them back, one wave went over them, and when they came up there were six still clinging to the boat; I counted them. The next wave turned the boat bottom upward, and emptied them all out. None of them ever came ashore alive. There were the rest of them all crowded together on the forecastle, the other parts of the ship being under water. They had seen all that happened to the boat. At length a heavy sea separated the forecastle from the rest of the wreck, and set it inside of the worst breaker, and the boat was able to reach them, and it saved all that were left, but one woman."

He also told us of the steamer *Cambria's* getting aground on his shore a few months before we were there, and of her English passengers who roamed over his grounds, and who, he said, thought the prospect from the high hill by the shore "the most delightsome they had ever seen," and also of the pranks which the ladies played with his scoop-net in the ponds. He spoke of these travellers with their purses full of guineas, just as our provincial fathers used to speak of British bloods in the time of King George the Third.

*Quid loquar?* Why repeat what he told us?

> "Aut Scyllam Nisi, quam fama secuta est,
> Candida succinctam latrantibus inguina monstris,
> Dulichias vexâsse rates, et gurgite in alto
> Ah timidos nautas canibus lacerâsse marinis?"

In the course of the evening I began to feel the potency of the clam which I had eaten, and I was obliged to confess to our host that I was no tougher than the cat he told of; but he answered, that he was a plain-spoken man, and he could tell me that it was all imagination. At any rate, it proved an emetic in my case, and I was made quite sick by it for a short time, while he laughed at my expense. I was pleased to read afterward, in Mourt's Relation of the landing of the Pilgrims in Provincetown Harbor, these words: "We found great muscles (the old editor says that they were undoubtedly sea-clams) and very fat and full of sea-pearl; but we could not eat them, for they made us all sick that did eat, as well sailors as passengers, ... but they were soon well again." It brought me nearer to the Pilgrims to be thus reminded by a similar experience that I was so like them. Moreover, it was a valuable confirmation of their story, and I am prepared now to believe every word of Mourt's Relation. I was also pleased to find that man and the clam lay still at the same angle to one another. But I did not notice sea-pearl. Like Cleopatra, I must have swallowed it. I have since dug these clams on a flat in the Bay and observed them. They could squirt full ten feet before the wind, as appeared by the marks of the drops on the sand.

"Now I'm going to ask you a question," said the old man, "and I don't know as you can tell me; but you are a learned man, and I never had any learning, only what I got by natur."—It was in vain that we reminded him that he could quote Josephus to our confusion.—"I've thought, if I ever met a learned man I should like to ask him this question. Can you tell me how *Axy* is spelt, and what it means? *Axy*," says he; "there's a girl over here is named *Axy*. Now what is it? What does it mean? Is it Scripture? I've read my Bible twenty-five years over and over, and I never came across it."

"Did you read it twenty-five years for this object.'" I asked.

"Well, *how* is it spelt? Wife, how is it spelt?" She said: "It is in the Bible; I've seen it."

"Well, how do you spell it?"

"I don't know. A c h, ach, s e h, seh,—Achseh."

"Does that spell Axy? Well, do *you* know what it means?" asked he, turning to me.

"No," I replied, "I never heard the sound before."

"There was a schoolmaster down here once, and they asked him what it meant, and he said it had no more meaning than a bean-pole."

I told him that I held the same opinion with the schoolmaster. I had been a schoolmaster myself, and had had strange names to deal with. I also heard of such names as Zoleth, Beriah, Amaziah, Bethuel, and Shearjashub, hereabouts.

At length the little boy, who had a seat quite in the chimney-corner, took off his stockings and shoes, warmed his feet, and having had his sore leg freshly salved, went off to bed; then the fool made bare his knotty-looking feet and legs, and followed him; and finally the old man exposed his calves also to our gaze. We had never had the good fortune to see an old man's legs before, and were surprised to find them fair and plump as an infant's, and we thought that he took a pride in exhibiting them. He then proceeded to make preparations for retiring, discoursing meanwhile with Panurgic plainness of speech on the ills to which old humanity is subject. We were a rare haul for him. He could commonly get none but ministers to talk to, though sometimes ten of them at once, and he was glad to meet some of the laity at leisure. The evening was not long enough for him. As I had been sick, the old lady asked if I would not go to bed,—it was getting late for old people; but the old man, who had not yet done his stories, said, "You ain't particular, are you?"

"O, no," said I, "I am in no hurry. I believe I have weathered the Clam cape."

"They are good," said he; "I wish I had some of them now."

"They never hurt me," said the old lady.

"But then you took out the part that killed a cat," said I.

At last we cut him short in the midst of his stories, which he promised to resume in the morning. Yet, after all, one of the old ladies who came into our room in the night to fasten the fire-board, which rattled, as she went out took the precaution to fasten us in. Old women are by nature more suspicious than old men. However, the winds howled around the house, and made the fire-boards as well as the casements rattle well that night. It was probably a windy night for any locality, but we could not distinguish the roar which was proper to the ocean from that which was due to the wind alone.

The sounds which the ocean makes must be very significant and interesting to those who live near it. When I was leaving the shore at this place the next summer, and had got a quarter of a mile distant, ascending a hill, I was startled by a sudden, loud sound from the sea, as if a large steamer were letting off steam by the shore, so that I caught my breath and felt my blood run cold for an instant, and I turned about, expecting to see one of the Atlantic steamers thus far out of her course, but there was nothing unusual to be seen. There was a low bank at the entrance of the Hollow, between me and the ocean, and suspecting that I might have risen into another stratum of air in ascending the hill,—which had wafted to me only the ordinary roar of the sea,—I immediately descended again, to see if I lost *hearing* of it; but, without regard to my ascending or descending, it died away in a minute or two, and yet there was scarcely any wind all the while. The old man said that this was what they called the "rut," a peculiar roar of the sea before the wind changes, which, however, he could not account for. He thought that he could tell all about the weather from the sounds which the sea made.

Old Josselyn, who came to New England in 1638, has it among his weather-signs, that "the resounding of the sea from the shore, and murmuring of the winds in the woods, without apparent wind, sheweth wind to follow."

Being on another part of the coast one night since this, I heard the roar of the surf a mile distant, and the inhabitants said it was a sign that the wind would work round east, and we should have rainy weather. The ocean was heaped up somewhere at the eastward, and this roar was occasioned by its effort to preserve its equilibrium, the wave reaching the shore before the wind. Also the captain of a packet between this country and England told me that he sometimes met with a wave on the Atlantic coming against the wind, perhaps in a calm sea, which indicated that at a distance the wind was blowing from an opposite quarter, but the undulation had travelled faster than it. Sailors tell of "tide-rips" and "ground-swells," which they suppose to have been occasioned by hurricanes and earthquakes, and to have travelled many hundred, and sometimes even two or three thousand miles.

Hunting for a Leak

Before sunrise the next morning they let us out again, and I ran over to the beach to see the sun come out of the ocean. The old woman of eighty-four winters was already out in the cold morning wind, bareheaded, tripping about like a young girl, and driving up the cow to milk. She got the breakfast with despatch, and without noise or bustle; and meanwhile the old man resumed his stories, standing before us, who were sitting, with his back to the chimney, and ejecting his tobacco juice right and left into the fire behind him, without regard to the various dishes which were there preparing. At breakfast we had eels, buttermilk cake, cold bread, green beans, doughnuts, and tea. The old man talked a steady stream; and when his wife told him he had better eat his breakfast, he said: "Don't hurry me; I have lived too long to be hurried." I ate of the apple-sauce and the doughnuts, which I thought had sustained the least detriment from the old man's shots, but my companion refused the apple-sauce, and ate of the hot cake and green beans, which had appeared to him to occupy the safest part of the hearth. But on comparing notes afterward, I told him that the buttermilk cake was particularly exposed, and I saw how it suffered repeatedly, and therefore I avoided it; but he declared that, however that might be, he witnessed that the apple-sauce was seriously injured, and had therefore declined that. After breakfast we looked at his clock, which was out of order, and oiled it with some "hen's grease," for want of sweet oil, for he scarcely could believe that we were not tinkers or pedlers; meanwhile he told a story about visions, which had reference to a crack in the clock-case made by frost one night. He was curious to know to what religious sect we belonged. He said that he had been to hear thirteen kinds of preaching in one month, when he was young, but he did not join any of them,—he stuck to his Bible. There was nothing like any of them in his Bible. While I was shaving in the next room, I heard him ask my companion to what sect he belonged, to which he answered:—

"O, I belong to the Universal Brotherhood."

"What's that?" he asked, "Sons o' Temperance?"

Finally, filling our pockets with doughnuts, which he was pleased to find that we called by the same name that he did, and paying for our entertainment, we took our departure; but he followed us out of doors, and made us tell him the names of the vegetables which he had raised from seeds that came out of the *Franklin*. They were cabbage, broccoli, and parsley. As I had asked him the names of so many things, he tried me in turn with all the plants which grew in his garden, both wild and cultivated. It was about half an acre, which he cultivated wholly himself. Besides the common garden vegetables, there were Yellow-Dock, Lemon Balm, Hyssop, Gill-go-over-the-ground. Mouse-ear, Chick-weed, Roman Wormwood, Elecampane, and other plants. As we stood there, I saw a fish-hawk stoop to pick a fish out of his pond.

"There," said I, "he has got a fish."

"Well," said the old man, who was looking all the while, but could see nothing, "he didn't dive, he just wet his claws."

And, sure enough, he did not this time, though it is said that they often do, but he merely stooped low enough to pick him out with his talons; but as he bore his shining prey over the bushes, it fell to the ground, and we did not see that he recovered it. That is not their practice.

Thus, having had another crack with the old man, he standing bareheaded under the eaves, he directed us "athwart the fields," and we took to the beach again for another day, it being now late in the morning.

It was but a day or two after this that the safe of the Provincetown Bank was broken open and robbed by two men from the interior, and we learned that our hospitable entertainers did at least transiently harbor the suspicion that we were the men.

## VI

### THE BEACH AGAIN

Our way to the high sand-bank, which I have described as extending all along the coast, led, as usual, through patches of Bayberry bushes which straggled into the sand. This, next to the Shrub-oak, was perhaps the most common shrub thereabouts. I was much attracted by its odoriferous leaves and small gray berries which are clustered about the short twigs, just below the last year's growth. I know of but two bushes in Concord, and they, being staminate plants, do not bear fruit. The berries gave it a venerable appearance, and they smelled quite spicy, like small confectionery. Robert Beverley, in his "History of Virginia," published in 1705, states that "at the mouth of their rivers, and all along upon the sea and bay, and near many of their creeks and swamps, grows the myrtle, bearing a berry, of which they make a hard brittle wax, of a curious green color, which by refining becomes almost transparent. Of this they make candles, which are never greasy to the touch nor melt with lying in the hottest weather; neither does the snuff of these ever offend the smell, like that of a tallow candle; but, instead of being disagreeable, if an accident puts a candle out, it yields a pleasant fragrancy to all that are in the room; insomuch that nice people often put them out on purpose to have the incense of the expiring snuff. The melting of these berries is said to have been first found out by a surgeon in New England, who performed wonderful things with a salve made of them." From the abundance of berries still hanging on the bushes, we judged that the inhabitants did not generally collect them for tallow, though we had seen a piece in the house we had just left. I have since made some tallow myself. Holding a basket beneath the bare twigs in April, I rubbed them together between my hands and thus gathered about a quart in twenty minutes, to which were added enough to make three pints, and I might have gathered them much faster with a suitable rake and a large shallow basket. They have little prominences like those of an orange all creased in tallow, which also fills the interstices down to the stone. The oily part rose to the top, making it look like a savory black broth, which smelled much like balm or other herb tea. You let it cool, then skim off the tallow from the surface, melt this again and strain it. I got about a quarter of a pound weight from my three pints, and more yet remained within the berries. A small portion cooled in the form of small flattish hemispheres, like crystallizations, the size of a kernel of corn (nuggets I called them as I picked them out from amid the berries), Loudon says, that "cultivated trees are said to yield more wax than those that are found wild." (See Duplessy, *Végetaux Résineux*, Vol. II. p. 60.) If you get any pitch on your hands in the pine-woods you have only to rub some of these berries between your hands to start it off. But the ocean was the grand fact there, which made us forget both bay berries and men.

To-day the air was beautifully clear, and the sea no longer dark and stormy, though the waves still broke with foam along the beach, but sparkling and full of life. Already that morning I had seen the day break over the sea as if it came out of its bosom:—

> "The saffron-robed Dawn rose in haste from the streams
> Of Ocean, that she might bring light to immortals and to mortals."

The sun rose visibly at such a distance over the sea that the cloud-bank in the horizon, which at first concealed him, was not perceptible until he had risen high behind it, and plainly broke and dispersed it, like an arrow. But as yet I looked at him as rising over land, and could not, without an effort, realize that he was rising over the sea. Already I saw some vessels on the horizon, which had rounded the Cape in the night, and were now well on their watery way to other lands.

We struck the beach again in the south part of Truro. In the early part of the day, while it was flood tide and the beach was narrow and soft, we walked on the bank, which was very high here, but not so level as the day before, being more interrupted by slight hollows. The author of the Description of the Eastern Coast says of this part, that "the bank is very high and steep. From the edge of it west, there is a strip of sand a hundred yards in breadth. Then succeeds low brushwood, a quarter of a mile wide, and almost impassable. After which comes a thick, perplexing forest, in which not a house is to be discovered. Seamen, therefore, though the distance between these two hollows (Newcomb's and Brush Hollows) is great, must not attempt to enter the wood, as in a snowstorm they must undoubtedly perish." This is still a true description of the country, except that there is not much high wood left.

Truro—Starting on a voyage

There were many vessels, like gulls, skimming over the surface of the sea, now half concealed in its troughs, their dolphin-strikers ploughing the water, now tossed on the top of the billows. One, a bark standing down parallel with the coast, suddenly furled her sails, came to anchor, and swung round in the wind, near us, only half a mile from the shore. At first we thought that her captain wished to communicate with us, and perhaps we did not regard the signal of distress, which a mariner would have understood, and he cursed us for cold-hearted wreckers who turned our backs on him. For hours we could still see her anchored there behind us, and we wondered how she could afford to loiter so long in her course. Or was she a smuggler who had chosen that wild beach to land her cargo on? Or did they wish to catch fish, or paint their vessel? Erelong other barks, and brigs, and schooners, which had in the mean while doubled the Cape, sailed by her in the smacking breeze, and our consciences were relieved. Some of these vessels lagged behind, while others steadily went ahead. We narrowly watched their rig, and the cut of their jibs, and how they walked the water, for there was all the difference between them that there is between living creatures. But we wondered that they should be remembering Boston and New York and Liverpool, steering for them, out there; as if the sailor might forget his peddling business on such a grand highway. They had perchance brought oranges from the Western Isles; and were they carrying back the peel? We might as well transport our old traps across the ocean of eternity. Is *that* but another "trading-flood," with its blessed isles? Is Heaven such a harbor as the Liverpool docks?

Still held on without a break, the inland barrens and shrubbery, the desert and the high sand bank with its even slope, the broad white beach, the breakers, the green water on the bar, and the Atlantic Ocean; and we traversed with delight new reaches of the shore; we took another lesson in sea-horses' manes and sea-cows' tails, in sea-jellies and sea-clams, with our new-gained experience. The sea ran hardly less than the day before. It seemed with every wave to be subsiding, because such was our expectation, and yet when hours had elapsed we could see no difference. But there it was, balancing itself, the restless ocean by our side, lurching in its gait. Each wave left the sand all braided or woven, as it were, with a coarse woof and warp, and a distinct raised edge to its rapid work. We made no haste, since we wished to see the ocean at our leisure; and indeed that soft sand was no place in which to be in a hurry, for one mile there was as good as two elsewhere. Besides, we were obliged frequently to empty our shoes of the sand which one took in in climbing or descending the bank.

As we were walking close to the water's edge this morning we turned round, by chance, and saw a large black object which the waves had just cast up on the beach behind us, yet too far off for us to distinguish what it was; and when we were about to return to it, two men came running from the bank, where no human beings had appeared before, as if they had come out of the sand, in order to save it before another wave took it. As we approached, it took successively the form of a huge fish, a drowned man, a sail or a net, and finally of a mass of towcloth, part of the cargo of the *Franklin*, which the men loaded into a cart.

Objects on the beach, whether men or inanimate things, look not only exceedingly grotesque, but much larger and more wonderful than they actually are. Lately, when approaching the seashore several degrees south of this, I saw before me, seemingly half a mile distant, what appeared like bold and rugged cliffs on the beach, fifteen feet high, and whitened by the sun and waves; but after a few steps it proved to be low heaps of rags,—part of the cargo of a wrecked vessel,—scarcely more than a foot in height. Once also it was my business to go in search of the relics of a human body, mangled by sharks, which had just been cast up, a week after a wreck, having got the direction from a light-house: I should find it a mile or two distant over the sand, a dozen rods from the water, covered with a cloth, by a stick stuck up. I expected that I must look very narrowly to find so small an object, but the sandy beach, half a mile wide, and stretching farther than the eye could reach, was so perfectly smooth and bare, and the mirage toward the sea so magnifying, that when I was half a mile distant the insignificant sliver which marked the spot looked like a bleached spar, and the relics were as conspicuous as if they lay in state on that sandy plain, or a generation had labored to pile up their cairn there. Close at hand they were simply some bones with a little flesh adhering to them, in fact, only a slight inequality in the sweep of the shore. There was nothing at all remarkable about them, and they were singularly inoffensive both to the senses and the imagination. But as I stood there they grew more and more imposing. They were alone with the beach and the sea, whose hollow roar seemed addressed to them, and I was impressed as if there was an understanding between them and the ocean which necessarily left me out, with my snivelling sympathies. That dead body had taken possession of the shore, and reigned over it as no living one, could, in the name of a certain majesty which belonged to it.

We afterward saw many small pieces of tow-cloth washed up, and I learn that it continued to be found in good condition, even as late as November in that year, half a dozen bolts at a time.

We eagerly filled our pockets with the smooth round pebbles which in some places, even here, were thinly sprinkled over the sand, together with flat circular shells (*Scutellæ?*); but, as we had read, when they were dry they had lost their beauty, and at each sitting we emptied our pockets again of the least remarkable, until our collection was well culled. Every material was rolled into the pebble form by. the waves; not only stones of various kinds, but the hard coal which some vessel had dropped, bits of glass, and in one instance a mass of peat three feet long, where there was nothing like it to be seen for many miles. All the great rivers of the globe are annually, if not constantly, discharging great quantities of lumber, which drifts to distant shores. I have also seen very perfect pebbles of brick, and bars of Castile soap from a wreck rolled into perfect cylinders, and still spirally streaked with red, like a barber's pole. When a cargo of rags is washed ashore, every old pocket and bag-like recess will be filled to bursting with sand by being rolled on the beach; and on one occasion, the pockets in the clothing of the wrecked being thus puffed up, even after they had been ripped open by wreckers, deluded me into the hope of identifying them by the contents. A pair of gloves looked exactly as if filled by a hand. The water in such clothing is soon wrung out and evaporated, but the sand, which works itself into every seam, is not so easily got rid of. Sponges, which are picked up on the shore, as is well known, retain some of the sand of the beach to the latest day, in spite of every effort to extract it.

I found one stone on the top of the bank, of a dark gray color, shaped exactly like a giant clam (*Mactra solidissima*), and of the same size; and, what was more remarkable, one-half of the outside had shelled off and lay near it, of the same form and depth with one of the valves of this clam, while the other half was loose, leaving a solid core of a darker color within it. I afterward saw a stone resembling a razor clam, but it was a solid one. It appeared as if the stone, in the process of formation, had filled the mould which a clam-shell furnished; or the same law that shaped the clam had made a clam of stone. Dead clams, with shells full of sand, are called sand clams. There were many of the large clamshells filled with sand; and sometimes one valve was separately filled exactly even, as if it had been heaped and then scraped. Even, among the many small stones on the top of the bank, I found one arrow-head.

Beside the giant clam and barnacles, we found on the shore a small clam (*Mesodesma arctata*), which I dug with my hands in numbers on the bars, and which is sometimes eaten by the inhabitants, in the absence of the *Mya arenaria*, on this side. Most of their empty shells had been perforated by some foe.—Also, the

*Astarte castanea.*

The Edible Mussel (*Mytilus edulis*) on the few rocks, and washed up in curious bunches of forty or fifty, held together by its rope-like *byssus*.

The Scollop Shell (*Pecten concentricus*), used for card-racks and pin-cushions.

Cockles, or Cuckoos (*Natica heros*), and their remarkable *nidus*, called "sand-circle," looking like the top of a stone jug without the stopple, and broken on one side, or like a flaring dickey made of sand-paper. Also,

*Cancellaria Couthouyi (?), and*

*Periwinkles (?) (Fusus decemcostatus).*

We afterward saw some other kinds on the Bay-side. Gould states that this Cape "has Hitler proved a barrier to the migrations of many species of Mollusca."—"Of the one hundred and ninety-seven species [which he described in 1840 as belonging to Massachusetts], eighty-three do not pass to the South shore, and fifty are not found on the North shore of the Cape."

Among Crustacea, there were the shells of Crabs and Lobsters, often bleached quite white high up the beach; Sea or Beach Fleas

(*Amphipoda*); and the cases of the Horse-shoe Crab, or Saucepan Fish (*Limulus Polyphemus*), of which we saw many alive on the Bay side, where they feed pigs on them. Their tails were used as arrow-heads by the Indians.

Of Radiata, there were the Sea Chestnut or Egg (*Echinus granulatus*), commonly divested of its spines; flat circular shells (*Scutella parma?*) covered with chocolate-colored spines, but becoming smooth and white, with five petal-like figures; a few Star-fishes or Five-fingers (*Asterias rubens*); and Sun-fishes or Sea-jellies (*Aureliæ*).

There was also at least one species of Sponge.

The plants which I noticed here and there on the pure sandy shelf, between the ordinary high-water mark and the foot of the bank, were Sea Rocket (*Cakile Americana*), Saltwort (*Salsola kali*), Sea Sandwort (*Honkenya peploides*), Sea Burdock (*Xanthium echinatum*), Sea-side Spurge (*Euphorbia poylgonifolia*); also, Beach Grass (*Arundo, Psamma,* or *Calamagrostis arenaria*), Sea-side Golden-rod (*Solidago sempervirens*), and the Beach Pea (*Lathyrus maritimus*).

Sometimes we helped a wrecker turn over a larger log than usual, or we amused ourselves with rolling stones down the bank, but we rarely could make one reach the water, the beach was so soft and wide; or we bathed in some shallow within a bar, where the sea covered us with sand at every flux, though it was quite cold and windy. The ocean there is commonly but a tantalizing prospect in hot weather, for with all that water before you, there is, as we were afterward told, no bathing on the Atlantic side, on account of the undertow and the rumor of sharks. At the lighthouse both in Eastham and Truro, the only houses quite on the shore, they declared, the next year, that they would not bathe there "for any sum," for they sometimes saw the sharks tossed up and quiver for a moment on the sand. Others laughed at these stories, but perhaps they could afford to because they never bathed anywhere. One old wrecker told us that he killed a regular man-eating shark fourteen feet long, and hauled him out with his oxen, where we had bathed; and another, that his father caught a smaller one of the same kind that was stranded there, by standing him up on his snout so that the waves could not take him. They will tell you tough stories of sharks all over the Cape, which I do not presume to doubt utterly,—how they will sometimes upset a boat, or tear it in pieces, to get at the man in it. I can easily believe in the undertow, but I have no doubt that one shark in a dozen years is enough to keep up the reputation of a beach a hundred miles long. I should add, however, that in July we walked on the bank here a quarter of a mile parallel with a fish about six feet in length, possibly a shark, which was prowling slowly along within two rods of the shore. It was of a pale brown color, singularly film-like and indistinct in the water, as if all nature abetted this child of ocean, and showed many darker transverse bars or rings whenever it came to the surface. It is well known that different fishes even of the same species are colored by the water they inhabit. We saw it go into a little cove or bathing-tub, where we had just been bathing, where the water was only four or five feet deep at that time, and after exploring it go slowly out again; but we continued to bathe there, only observing first from the bank if the cove was preoccupied. We thought that the water was fuller of life, more aerated perhaps than that of the Bay, like soda-water, for we were as particular as young salmon, and the expectation of encountering a shark did not subtract anything from its life-giving qualities.

Sometimes we sat on the wet beach and watched the beach birds, sand-pipers, and others, trotting along close to each wave, and waiting for the sea to cast up their breakfast. The former (*Charadrius melodus*) ran with great rapidity and then stood stock still remarkably erect and hardly to be distinguished from the beach. The wet sand was covered with small skipping Sea Fleas, which apparently make a part of their food. These last are the little scavengers of the beach, and are so numerous that they will devour large fishes, which have been cast up, in a very short time. One little bird not larger than a sparrow,—it may have been a Phalarope,—would alight on the turbulent surface where the breakers were five or six feet high, and float buoyantly there like a duck, cunningly taking to its wings and lifting itself a few feet through the air over the foaming crest of each breaker, but sometimes outriding safely a considerable billow which hid it some seconds, when its instinct told it that it would not break. It was a little creature thus to sport with the ocean, but it was as perfect a success in its way as the breakers in theirs. There was also an almost uninterrupted line of coots rising and falling with the waves, a few rods from the shore, the whole length of the Cape. They made as constant a part of the ocean's border as the pads or pickerel-weed do of that of a pond. We read the following as to the Storm Petrel (*Thalassidroma Wilsonii*), which is seen in the Bay as well as on the outside. "The feathers on the breast of the Storm Petrel are, like those of all swimming birds, water-proof; but substances not susceptible of being wetted with water are, for that very reason, the best fitted for collecting oil from its surface. That function is performed by the feathers on the breast of the Storm Petrels as they touch on the surface; and though that may not be the only way in which they procure their food, it is certainly that in which they obtain great part of it. They dash along till they have loaded their feathers and then they pause upon the wave and remove the oil with their bills."

Thus we kept on along the gently curving shore, seeing two or three miles ahead at once,—along this ocean side-walk, where there was none to turn out for, with the middle of the road the highway of nations on our right, and the sand cliffs of the Cape on our left. We saw this forenoon a part of the wreck of a vessel, probably the *Franklin*, a large piece fifteen feet square, and still freshly painted. With a grapple and a line we could have saved it, for the waves repeatedly washed it within cast, but they as often took it back. It would have been a lucky haul for some poor wrecker, for I have been told that one man who paid three or four dollars for a part of the wreck of that vessel, sold fifty or sixty dollars' worth of iron out of it. Another, the same who picked up the Captain's valise with the memorable letter in it, showed me, growing in his garden, many pear and plum trees which washed ashore from her, all nicely tied up and labelled, and he said that he might have got five hundred dollars' worth; for a Mr. Bell was importing the nucleus of a nursery to be established near Boston. His turnip-seed came from the same source. Also valuable spars from the same vessel and from the *Cactus* lay in his yard. In short the inhabitants visit the beach to see what they have caught as regularly as a fisherman his weir or a lumberer his boom; the Cape is their boom. I heard of one who had recently picked up twenty barrels of apples in good condition, probably a part of a deck load thrown over in a storm.

Though there are wreck-masters appointed to look after valuable property which must be advertised, yet undoubtedly a great deal of value is secretly carried off. But are we not all wreckers contriving that some treasure may be washed up on our beach, that we may secure it, and do we not infer the habits of these Nauset and Barnegat wreckers from the common modes of getting a living?

The sea, vast and wild as it is, bears thus the waste and wrecks of human art to its remotest shore. There is no telling what it may not vomit up. It lets nothing lie; not even the giant clams which cling to its bottom. It is still heaving up the tow-cloth of the *Franklin*, and perhaps a piece of some old pirate's ship, wrecked more than a hundred years ago, comes ashore to-day. Some years since, when a vessel was wrecked here which had nutmegs in her cargo, they were strewn all along the beach, and for a considerable time were not spoiled by the salt water. Soon afterward, a fisherman caught a cod which was full of them. Why, then, might not the Spice-Islanders shake their nutmeg trees into the ocean, and let all nations who stand in need of them pick them up? However, after a year, I found that the nutmegs from the *Franklin* had become soft.

You might make a curious list of articles which fishes have swallowed,—sailors' open clasp-knives, and bright tin snuff-boxes, not knowing what was in them,—and jugs, and jewels, and Jonah. The other day I came across the following scrap in a newspaper.

> "A Religious Fish.—A short time ago, mine host Stewart, of the Denton Hotel, purchased a rockfish, weighing about sixty pounds. On opening it he found in it a certificate of membership of the M. E. Church, which we read as follows:—

Member
    Methodist E. Church.
        Founded A. D. 1784.

Quarterly Ticket.
>18
>Minister.

'For our light affliction, which is but for a moment, worketh for us a far more exceeding and eternal weight of glory.'—2 Cor. iv. 17.

'O what are all my sufferings here,
  If, Lord, thou count me meet
With that enraptured host t' appear,
  And worship at thy feet!'

"The paper was of course in a crumpled and wet condition, but on exposing it to the sun, and ironing the kinks out of it, it became quite legible.—*Denton (Md.) Journal.*"

From time to time we saved a wreck ourselves, a box or barrel, and set it on its end, and appropriated it with crossed sticks; and it will lie there perhaps, respected by brother wreckers, until some more violent storm shall take it, really lost to man until wrecked again. We also saved, at the cost of wet feet only, a valuable cord and buoy, part of a seine, with which the sea was playing, for it seemed ungracious to refuse the least gift which so great a personage offered you. We brought this home and still use it for a garden line. I picked up a bottle half buried in the wet sand, covered with barnacles, but stoppled tight, and half full of red ale, which still smacked of juniper,—all that remained I fancied from the wreck of a rowdy world,—that great salt sea on the one hand, and this little sea of ale on the other, preserving their separate characters. What if it could tell us its adventures over countless ocean waves! Man would not be man through such ordeals as it had passed. But as I poured it slowly out on to the sand, it seemed to me that man himself was like a half-emptied bottle of pale ale, which Time had drunk so far, yet stoppled tight for a while, and drifting about in the ocean of circumstances; but destined erelong to mingle with the surrounding waves, or be spilled amid the sands of a distant shore.

In the summer I saw two men fishing for Bass hereabouts. Their bait was a bullfrog, or several small frogs in a bunch, for want of squid. They followed a retiring wave and whirling their lines round and round their heads with increasing rapidity, threw them as far as they could into the sea; then retreating, sat down, flat on the sand, and waited for a bite. It was literally (or *littorally*) walking down to the shore, and throwing your line into the Atlantic. I should not have known what might take hold of the other end, whether Proteus or another. At any rate, if you could not pull him in, why, you might let him go without being pulled in yourself. And *they* knew by experience that it would be a Striped Bass, or perhaps a Cod, for these fishes play along near the shore.

From time to time we sat under the lee of a sand-hill on the bank, thinly covered with coarse Beach-grass, and steadily gazed on the sea, or watched the vessels going south, all Blessings of the Bay of course. We could see a little more than half a circle of ocean, besides the glimpses of the Bay which we got behind us; the sea there was not wild and dreary in all respects, for there were frequently a hundred sail in sight at once on the Atlantic. You can commonly count about eighty in a favorable summer day and pilots sometimes land and ascend the bank to look out for these which require their services. These had been waiting for fair weather, and had come out of Boston Harbor together. The same is the case when they have been assembled in the Vineyard Sound, so that you may see but few one day, and a large fleet the next. Schooners with many jibs and stay-sails crowded all the sea road; square-rigged vessels with their great height and breadth of canvas were ever and anon appearing out of the far horizon, or disappearing and sinking into it; here and there a pilot-boat was towing its little boat astern toward some distant foreigner who had just fired a gun, the echo of which along the shore sounded like the caving of the bank. We could see the pilot looking through his glass toward the distant ship which was putting back to speak with him. He sails many a mile to meet her; and now she puts her sails aback, and communicates with him alongside,—sends some important message to the owners, and then bids farewell to these shores for good and all; or, perchance a propeller passed and made fast to some disabled craft, or one that had been becalmed, whose cargo of fruit might spoil. Though silently, and for the most part incommunicatively, going about their business, they were, no doubt, a source of cheerfulness and a kind of society to one another.

Unloading the day's catch

To-day it was the Purple Sea, an epithet which I should not before have accepted. There were distinct patches of the color of a purple grape with the bloom rubbed off. But first and last the sea is of all colors. Well writes Gilpin concerning "the brilliant hues which are continually playing on the surface of a quiet ocean," and this was not too turbulent at a distance from the shore. "Beautiful," says he, "no doubt in a high degree are those glimmering tints which often invest the tops of mountains; but they are mere coruscations compared with these marine colors, which are continually varying and shifting into each other in all the vivid splendor of the rainbow, through the space often of several leagues." Commonly, in calm weather, for half a mile from the shore, where the bottom tinges it, the sea is green, or greenish, as are some ponds; then blue for many miles, often with purple tinges, bounded in the distance by a light almost silvery stripe; beyond which there is generally a dark-blue rim, like a mountain-ridge in the horizon, as if, like that, it owed its color to the intervening atmosphere. On another day it will be marked with long streaks, alternately smooth and rippled, light-colored and dark, even like our inland meadows in a freshet, and showing which way the wind sets.

Thus we sat on the foaming shore, looking on the wine-colored ocean,—

Φίν᾽ ἔφ᾽ ἁλὸς πολιῆς, ὁρόων ἐπὶ οἴνοπα πόντον.

Here and there was a darker spot on its surface, the shadow of a cloud, though the sky was so clear that no cloud would have been noticed otherwise, and no shadow would have been seen on the land, where a much smaller surface is visible at once. So, distant clouds and showers may be seen on all sides by a sailor in the course of a day, which do not necessarily portend rain where he is. In July we saw similar dark-blue patches where schools of Menhaden rippled the surface, scarcely to be distinguished from the shadows of clouds. Sometimes the sea was spotted with them far and wide, such is its inexhaustible fertility. Close at hand you see their back fin, which is very long and sharp, projecting two or three inches above water. From time to time also we saw the white bellies of the Bass playing along the shore.

It was a poetic recreation to watch those distant sails steering for half-fabulous ports, whose very names are a mysterious music to our ears: Fayal, and Babelmandel, ay, and Chagres, and Panama,—bound to the famous Bay of San Francisco, and the golden streams of Sacramento and San Joaquin, to Feather River and the American Fork, where Sutter's Fort presides, and inland stands the City de los Angeles. It is remarkable that men do not sail the sea with more expectation. Nothing remarkable was ever accomplished in a prosaic mood. The heroes and discoverers have found true more than was previously believed, only when they were expecting and dreaming of something more than their contemporaries dreamed of, or even themselves discovered, that is, when they were in a frame of mind fitted to behold the truth. Referred to the world's standard, they are always insane. Even savages have indirectly surmised as much. Humboldt, speaking of Columbus approaching the New World, says: "The grateful coolness of the evening air, the ethereal purity of the starry firmament, the balmy fragrance of flowers, wafted to him by the land breeze, all led him to suppose (as we are told by Herrara, in the Decades) that he was approaching the garden of Eden, the sacred abode of our first parents. The Orinoco seemed to him one of the four rivers which, according to the venerable tradition of the ancient world, flowed from Paradise, to water and divide the surface of the earth, newly adorned with plants." So even the expeditions for the discovery of El Dorado, and of the Fountain of Youth, led to real, if not compensatory discoveries.

We discerned vessels so far off, when once we began to look, that only the tops of their masts in the horizon were visible, and it took a strong intention of the eye, and its most favorable side, to see them at all, and sometimes we doubted if we were not counting our eyelashes. Charles Darwin states that he saw, from the base of the Andes, "the masts of the vessels at anchor in the bay of Valparaiso, although not less than twenty-six geographical miles distant," and that Anson had been surprised at the distance at which his vessels were discovered from the coast, without knowing the reason, namely, the great height of the land and the transparency of the air. Steamers may be detected much farther than sailing vessels, for, as one says, when their hulls and masts of wood and iron are down, their smoky masts and streamers still betray them; and the same writer, speaking of the comparative advantages of bituminous and anthracite coal for war-steamers, states that, "from the ascent of the columns of smoke above the horizon, the motions of the steamers in Calais Harbor [on the coast of France] are at all times observable at Ramsgate [on the English coast], from the first lighting of the fires to the putting out at sea; and that in America the steamers burning the fat bituminous coal can be tracked at sea at least seventy miles before the hulls become visible, by the dense columns of black smoke pouring out of their chimneys, and trailing along the horizon."

Though there were numerous vessels at this great distance in the horizon on every side, yet the vast spaces between them, like the spaces between the stars, far as they were distant from us, so were they from one another,—nay, some were twice as far from each other as from us,—impressed us with a sense of the immensity of the ocean, the "unfruitful ocean," as it has been called, and we could see what proportion man and his works bear to the globe. As we looked off, and saw the water growing darker and darker and deeper and deeper the farther we looked, till it was awful to consider, and it appeared to have no relation to the friendly land, either as shore or bottom,—of what use is a bottom if it is out of sight, if it is two or three miles from the surface, and you are to be drowned so long before you get to it, though it were made of the same stuff with your native soil?—over that ocean, where, as the Veda says, "there is nothing to give support, nothing to rest upon, nothing to cling to," I felt that I was a land animal. The man in a balloon even may commonly alight on the earth in a few moments, but the sailor's only hope is that he may reach the distant shore. I could then appreciate the heroism of the old navigator. Sir Humphrey Gilbert, of whom it is related that, being overtaken by a storm when on his return from America, in the year 1583, far northeastward from where we were, sitting abaft with a book in his hand, just before he was swallowed up in the deep, he cried out to his comrades in the *Hind*, as they came within hearing, "We are as near to Heaven by sea as by land." I saw that it would not be easy to realize.

On Cape Cod, the next most eastern land you hear of is St. George's Bank (the fishermen tell of "Georges," "Cashus," and other sunken lands which they frequent). Every Cape man has a theory about George's Bank having been an island once, and in their accounts they gradually reduce the shallowness from six, five, four, two fathoms, to somebody's confident assertion that he has seen a mackerel-gull sitting; on a piece of dry land there. It reminded me, when I thought of the shipwrecks which had taken place there, of the Isle of Demons, laid down off this coast in old charts of the New World. There must be something monstrous, methinks, in a vision of the sea bottom from over some bank a thousand miles from the shore, more awful than its imagined bottomlessness; a drowned continent, all livid and frothing at the nostrils, like the body of a drowned man, which is better sunk deep than near the surface.

I have been surprised to discover from a steamer the shallowness of Massachusetts Bay itself. Off Billingsgate Point I could have touched the bottom with a pole, and I plainly saw it variously shaded with seaweed, at five or six miles from the shore. This is "The Shoal-ground of the Cape," it is true, but elsewhere the bay is not much deeper than a country pond. We are told that the deepest water in the English Channel between Shakespeare's Cliff and Cape Grinéz, in France, is one hundred and eighty feet; and Guyot says that "the Baltic Sea has a depth of only one hundred and twenty feet between the coasts of Germany and those of Sweden," and "the Adriatic between Venice and Trieste has a depth of only one hundred and thirty feet." A pond in my native town, only half a mile long, is more than one hundred feet deep.

The ocean is but a larger lake. At midsummer you may sometimes see a strip of glassy smoothness on it, a few rods in width and many miles long, as if the surface there were covered with a thin pellicle of oil, just as on a country pond; a sort of stand-still, you would say, at the meeting or parting of two currents of air (if it does not rather mark the unrippled steadiness of a current of water beneath), for sailors tell of the ocean and land breeze meeting between the fore and aft sails of a vessel, while the latter are full, the former being suddenly taken aback. Daniel Webster, in one of his letters describing blue-fishing off

Martha's Vineyard, referring to those smooth places, which fishermen and sailors call "slicks," says: "We met with them yesterday, and our boatman made for them, whenever discovered. He said they were caused by the blue-fish chopping up their prey. That is to say, those voracious fellows get into a school of menhaden, which are too large to swallow whole, and they bite them into pieces to suit their tastes. And the oil from this butchery, rising to the surface, makes the 'slick.'"

Yet this same placid Ocean, as civil now as a city's harbor, a place for ships and commerce, will erelong be lashed into sudden fury, and all its caves and cliffs will resound with tumult. It will ruthlessly heave these vessels to and fro, break them in pieces in its sandy or stony jaws, and deliver their crews to sea-monsters. It will play with them like seaweed, distend them like dead frogs, and carry them about, now high, now low, to show to the fishes, giving them a nibble. This gentle Ocean will toss and tear the rag of a man's body like the father of mad bulls, and his relatives may be seen seeking the remnants for weeks along the strand. From some quiet inland hamlet they have rushed weeping to the unheard-of shore, and now stand uncertain where a sailor has recently been buried amid the sandhills.

It is generally supposed that they who have long been conversant with the Ocean can foretell by certain indications, such as its roar and the notes of sea-fowl, when it will change from calm to storm; but probably no such ancient mariner as we dream of exists; they know no more, at least, than the older sailors do about this voyage of life on which we are all embarked. Nevertheless, we love to hear the sayings of old sailors, and their accounts of natural phenomena, which totally ignore, and are ignored by, science; and possibly they have not always looked over the gunwale so long in vain. Kalm repeats a story which was told him in Philadelphia by a Mr. Cock, who was one day sailing to the West Indies in a small yacht, with an old man on board who was well acquainted with those seas. "The old man sounding the depth, called to the mate to tell Mr. Cock to launch the boats immediately, and to put a sufficient number of men into them, in order to tow the yacht during the calm, that they might reach the island before them as soon as possible, as within twenty-four hours there would be a strong hurricane. Mr. Cock asked him what reasons he had to think so; the old man replied that, on sounding, he saw the lead in the water at a distance of many fathoms more than he had seen it before; that therefore the water was become clear all of a sudden, which he looked upon as a certain sign of an impending hurricane in the sea." The sequel of the story is that, by good fortune and by dint of rowing they managed to gain a safe harbor before the hurricane had reached its height; but it finally raged with so much violence that not only many ships were lost and houses unroofed, but even their own vessel in harbor was washed so far on shore that several weeks elapsed before it could be got off.

The Greeks would not have called the ocean ἀτρύγετος, or unfruitful, though it does not produce wheat, if they had viewed it by the light of modern science; for naturalists now assert that "the sea, and not the land, is the principal seat of life,"—though not of vegetable life. Darwin affirms that "our most thickly inhabited forests appear almost as deserts when we come to compare them with the corresponding regions of the ocean." Agassiz and Gould tell us that "the sea teems with animals of all classes, far beyond the extreme point of flowering plants"; but they add that "experiments of dredging in very deep water have also taught us that the abyss of the ocean is nearly a desert";—"so that modern investigations," to quote the words of Desor, "merely go to confirm the great idea which was vaguely anticipated by the ancient poets and philosophers, that the Ocean is the origin of all things." Yet marine animals and plants hold a lower rank in the scale of being than land animals and plants. "There is no instance known," says Desor, "of an animal becoming aquatic in its perfect state, after having lived in its lower stage on dry land." but as in the case of the tadpole, "the progress invariably points towards the dry land." In short, the dry land itself came through and out of the water in its way to the heavens, for, "in going back through the geological ages, we come to an epoch when, according to all appearances, the dry land did not exist, and when the surface of our globe was entirely covered with water." We looked on the sea, then, once more, not as ἀτρύγετος, or unfruitful, but as it has been more truly called, the "laboratory of continents."

Though we have indulged in some placid reflections of late, the reader must not forget that the dash and roar of the waves were incessant. Indeed, it would be well if he were to read with a large conch-shell at his ear. But notwithstanding that it was very cold and windy to-day, it was such a cold as we thought would not cause one to take cold who was exposed to it, owing to the saltness of the air and the dryness of the soil. Yet the author of the old Description of Wellfleet says: "The atmosphere is very much impregnated with saline particles, which, perhaps, with the great use of fish, and the neglect of cider and spruce-beer, may be a reason why the people are more subject to sore mouths and throats than in other places."

## VII

### ACROSS THE CAPE

When we have returned from the seaside, we sometimes ask ourselves why we did not spend more time in gazing at the sea; but very soon the traveller does not look as the sea more than at the heavens. As for the interior, if the elevated sand-bar in the midst of the ocean can be said to have any interior, it was an exceedingly desolate landscape, with rarely a cultivated or cultivable field in sight. We saw no villages, and seldom a house, for these are generally on the Bay side. It was a succession of shrubby hills and valleys, now wearing an autumnal tint. You would frequently think, from the character of the surface, the dwarfish trees, and the bearberries around, that you were on the top of a mountain. The only wood in Eastham was on the edge of Wellfleet. The pitch-pines were not commonly more than fifteen or eighteen feet high. The larger ones covered with lichens,—often hung with the long gray *Usnea*. There is scarcely a white-pine on the forearm of the Cape. Yet in the northwest part of Eastham, near the Camp Ground, we saw, the next summer, some quite rural, and even sylvan retreats, for the Cape, where small rustling groves of oaks and locusts and whispering pines, on perfectly level ground, made a little paradise. The locusts, both transplanted and growing naturally about the houses there, appeared to flourish better than any other tree. There were thin belts of wood in Wellfleet and Truro, a mile or more from the Atlantic, but, for the most part, we could see the horizon through them, or, if extensive, the trees were not large. Both oaks and pines had often the same flat look with the apple-trees. Commonly, the oak woods twenty-five years old were a mere scraggy shrubbery nine or ten feet high, and we could frequently reach to their topmost leaf. Much that is called "woods" was about half as high as this,—only patches of shrub-oak, bayberry, beach-plum, and wild roses, overrun with woodbine. When the roses were in bloom, these patches in the midst of the sand displayed such a profusion of blossoms, mingled with the aroma of the bayberry, that no Italian or other artificial rose-garden could equal them. They were perfectly Elysian, and realized my idea of an oasis in the desert. Huckleberry-bushes were very abundant, and the next summer they bore a remarkable quantity of that kind of gall called Huckleberry-apple, forming quite handsome though monstrous blossoms. But it must be added, that this shrubbery swarmed with wood-ticks, sometimes very troublesome parasites, and which it takes very horny fingers to crack.

A Truro footpath

The inhabitants of these towns have a great regard for a tree, though their standard for one is necessarily neither large nor high; and when they tell you of the large trees that once grew here, you must think of them, not as absolutely large, but large compared with the present generation. Their "brave old oaks," of which they speak with so much respect, and which they will point out to you as relics of the primitive forest, one hundred or one hundred and fifty, ay, for aught they know, two hundred years old, have a ridiculously dwarfish appearance, which excites a smile in the beholder. The largest and most venerable which they will show you in such a case are, perhaps, not more than twenty or twenty-five feet high. I was especially amused by the Liliputian old oaks in the south part of Truro. To the inexperienced eye, which appreciated their proportions only, they might appear vast as the tree which saved his royal majesty, but measured, they were dwarfed at once almost into lichens which a deer might eat up in a morning. Yet they will tell you that large schooners were once built of timber which grew in Wellfleet. The old houses also are built of the timber of the Cape; but instead of the forests in the midst of which they originally stood, barren heaths, with poverty-grass for heather, now stretch away on every side. The modern houses are built of what is called "dimension timber," *imported* from Maine, all ready to be set up, so that commonly they do not touch it again with an axe. Almost all the wood used for fuel is imported by vessels or currents, and of course all the coal. I was told that probably a quarter of the fuel and a considerable part of the lumber used in North Truro was drift-wood. Many get *all* their fuel from the beach.

Of birds not found in the interior of the State,—at least in my neighborhood,—I heard, in the summer, the Black-throated Bunting (*Fringilla Americana*) amid the shrubbery, and in the open land the Upland Plover (*Totanus Bartramius*), whose quivering notes were ever and anon prolonged into a clear, somewhat plaintive, yet hawk-like scream, which sounded at a very indefinite distance. The bird may have been in the next field, though it sounded a mile off.

To-day we were walking through Truro, a town of about eighteen hundred inhabitants. We had already come to Pamet River, which empties into the Bay. This was the limit of the Pilgrims' journey up the Cape from Provincetown, when seeking a place for settlement. It rises in a hollow within a few rods of the Atlantic, and one who lives near its source told us that in high tides the sea leaked through, yet the wind and waves preserve intact the barrier between them, and thus the whole river is steadily driven westward butt-end foremost,—fountain-head, channel, and light-house at the mouth, all together.

Early in the afternoon we reached the Highland Light, whose white tower we had seen rising out of the bank in front of us for the last mile or two. It is fourteen miles from the Nauset Lights, on what is called the Clay Pounds, an immense bed of clay abutting on the Atlantic, and, as the keeper told us, stretching quite across the Cape, which is here only about two miles wide. We perceived at once a difference in the soil, for there was an interruption of the desert, and a slight appearance of a sod under our feet, such as we had not seen for the last two days.

After arranging to lodge at the light-house, we rambled across the Cape to the Bay, over a singularly bleak and barren-looking country, consisting of rounded hills and hollows, called by geologists diluvial elevations and depressions,—a kind of scenery which has been compared to a chopped sea, though this suggests too sudden a transition. There is a delineation of this very landscape in Hitchcock's Report on the Geology of Massachusetts, a work which, by its size at least, reminds one of a diluvial elevation itself. Looking southward from the light-house, the Cape appeared like an elevated plateau, sloping very regularly, though slightly, downward from the edge of the bank on the Atlantic side, about one hundred and fifty feet above the ocean, to that on the Bay side. On traversing this we found it to be interrupted by broad valleys or gullies, which become the hollows in the bank when the sea has worn up to them. They are commonly at right angles with the shore, and often extend quite across the Cape. Some of the valleys, however, are circular, a hundred feet deep without any outlet, as if the Cape had sunk in those places, or its sands had run out. The few scattered houses which we passed, being placed at the bottom of the hollows for shelter and fertility, were, for the most part, concealed entirely, as much as if they had been swallowed up in the earth. Even a village with its meeting-house, which we had left little more than a stone's throw behind, had sunk into the earth, spire and all, and we saw only the surface of the upland and the sea on either hand. When approaching it, we had mistaken the belfry for a summer-house on the plain. We began to think that we might tumble into a village before we were aware of it, as into an ant-lion's hole, and be drawn into the sand irrecoverably. The most conspicuous objects on the land were a distant windmill, or a meeting-house standing alone, for only they could afford to occupy an exposed place. A great part of the township, however, is a barren, heath-like plain, and perhaps one third of it lies in common, though the property of individuals. The author of the old "Description of Truro," speaking of the soil, says: "The snow, which would be of essential service to it provided it lay level and covered the ground, is blown into drifts and into the sea." This peculiar open country, with here and there a patch of shrubbery, extends as much as seven miles, or from Pamet River on the south to High Head on the north, and from Ocean to Bay. To walk over it makes on a stranger such an impression as being at sea, and he finds it impossible to estimate distances in any weather. A windmill or a herd of cows may seem to be far away in the horizon, yet, after going a few rods, he will be close upon them. He is also deluded by other kinds of mirage. When, in the summer, I saw a family a-blueberrying a mile off, walking about amid the dwarfish bushes which did not come up higher than their ankles, they seemed to me to be a race of giants, twenty feet high at least.

The highest and sandiest portion next the Atlantic was thinly covered with Beach-grass and Indigo-weed. Next to this the surface of the upland generally consisted of white sand and gravel, like coarse salt, through which a scanty vegetation found its way up. It will give an ornithologist some idea of its barrenness if I mention that the next June, the month of grass. I found a night-hawk's eggs there, and that almost any square rod thereabouts, taken at random, would be an eligible site for such a deposit. The kildeer-plover, which loves a similar locality, also drops its eggs there, and fills the air above with its din. This upland also produced *Cladonia* lichens, poverty-grass, savory-leaved aster (*Diplopappus linariifolius*), mouse-ear, bear-berry, &c. On a few hillsides the savory-leaved aster and mouse-ear alone made quite a dense sward, said to be very pretty when the aster is in bloom. In some parts the two species of poverty-grass (*Hudsonia tomentosa* and *ericoides*), which deserve a better name, reign for miles in littli hemispherical tufts or islets, like moss, scattered over the waste. They linger in bloom there till the middle of July. Occasionally near the beach these rounded beds, as also those of the sea-sandwort (*Honkenya peploides*), were filled with sand within an inch of their tops, and were hard, like large ant-hills, while the surrounding sand was soft. In summer, if the poverty-grass grows at the head of a Hollow looking toward the sea, in a bleak position where the wind rushes up, the northern or exposed half of the tuft is sometimes all black and dead like an oven-broom, while the opposite half is yellow with blossoms, the whole hillside thus presenting a remarkable contrast when seen from the poverty-stricken and the flourishing side. This plant, which in many places would be esteemed an ornament, is here despised by many on account of its being associated with barrenness. It might well be adopted for the Barnstable coat-of-arms, in a field *sableux*. I should be proud of it. Here and there were tracts of Beach-grass mingled with the Sea-side Goldenrod and Beach-pea, which reminded us still more forcibly of the ocean.

Truro meeting-house on the hill

We read that there was not a brook in Truro. Yet there were deer here once, which must often have panted in vain; but I am pretty sure that I afterward saw a small fresh-water brook emptying into the south side of Pamet River, though I was so heedless as not to taste it. At any rate, a little boy near by told me that he drank at it. There was not a tree as far as we could see, and that was many miles each way, the general level of the upland being about the same everywhere. Even from the Atlantic side we overlooked the Bay, and saw to Manomet Point in Plymouth, and better from that side because it was the highest. The almost universal bareness and smoothness of the landscape were as agreeable as novel, making it so much the more like the deck of a vessel. We saw vessels sailing south into the Bay, on the one hand, and north along the Atlantic shore, on the other, all with an aft wind.

The single road which runs lengthwise the Cape, now winding over the plain, now through the shrubbery which scrapes the wheels of the stage, was a mere cart-track in the sand, commonly without any fences to confine it, and continually changing from this side to that, to harder ground, or sometimes to avoid the tide. But the inhabitants travel the waste here and there pilgrim-wise and staff in hand, by narrow footpaths, through which the sand flows out and reveals the nakedness of the land. We shuddered at the thought of living there and taking our afternoon walks over those barren swells, where we could overlook every step of our walk before taking it, and would have to pray for a fog or a snow-storm to conceal our destiny. The walker there must soon eat his heart.

In the north part of the town there is no house from shore to shore for several miles, and it is as wild and solitary as the Western Prairies— used to be. Indeed, one who has seen every house in Truro will be surprised to hear of the number of the inhabitants, but perhaps five hundred of the men and boys of this small town were then abroad on their fishing grounds. Only a few men stay at home to till the sand or watch for blackfish. The farmers are fishermen-farmers and understand better ploughing the sea than the land. They do not disturb their sands much, though there is a plenty of sea-weed in the creeks, to say nothing of blackfish occasionally rotting the shore. Between the Pond and East Harbor Village there was an interesting plantation of pitch-pines, twenty or thirty acres in extent, like those which we had already seen from the stage. One who lived near said that the land was purchased by two men for a shilling or twenty-five cents an acre. Some is not considered worth writing a deed for. This soil or sand, which was partially covered with poverty and beach grass, sorrel, &c., was furrowed at intervals of about four feet and the seed dropped by a machine. The pines had come up admirably and grown the first year three or four inches, and the second six inches and more. Where the seed had been lately planted the white sand was freshly exposed in an endless furrow winding round and round the sides of the deep hollows, in a vertical spiral manner, which produced a very singular effect, as if you were looking into the reverse side of a vast banded shield. This experiment, so important to the Cape, appeared very successful, and perhaps the time will come when the greater part of this kind of land in Barnstable County will be thus covered with an artificial pine forest, as has been done in some parts of France. In that country 12,500 acres of downs had been thus covered in 1811 near Bayonne. They are called *pignadas*, and according to Loudon "constitute the principal riches of the inhabitants, where there was a drifting desert before." It seemed a nobler kind of grain to raise than corn even.

A herd of cows

A few years ago Truro was remarkable among the Cape towns for the number of sheep raised in it; but I was told that at this time only two men kept sheep in the town, and in 1855, a Truro boy ten years old told me that he had never seen one. They were formerly pastured on the unfenced lands or general fields, but now the owners were more particular to assert their rights, and it cost too much for fencing. The rails are cedar from Maine, and two rails will answer for ordinary purposes, but four are required for sheep. This was the reason assigned by one who had formerly kept them for not keeping them any longer. Fencing stuff is so expensive that I saw fences made with only one rail, and very often the rail when split was carefully tied with a string. In one of the villages I saw the next summer a cow tethered by a rope six rods long, the rope long in proportion as the feed was short and thin. Sixty rods, ay, all the cables of the Cape, would have been no more than fair. Tethered in the desert for fear that she would get into Arabia Felix! I helped a man weigh a bundle of hay which he was selling to his neighbor, holding one end of a pole from which it swung by a steel-yard hook, and this was just half his whole crop. In short, the country looked so barren that I several times refrained from asking the inhabitants for a string or a piece of wrapping-paper, for fear I should rob them, for they plainly were obliged to import these things as well as rails, and where there were no newsboys, I did not see what they would do for waste paper.

The objects around us, the make-shifts of fishermen ashore, often made us look down to see if we were standing on terra firma. In the wells everywhere a block and tackle were used to raise the bucket, instead of a windlass, and by almost every house was laid up a spar or a plank or two full of auger-holes, saved from a wreck. The windmills were partly built of these, and they were worked into the public bridges. The light-house keeper, who was having his barn shingled, told me casually that he had made three thousand good shingles for that purpose out of a mast. You would sometimes see an old oar used for a rail. Frequently also some fair-weather finery ripped off a vessel by a storm near the coast was nailed up against an outhouse. I saw fastened to a shed near the lighthouse a long new sign with the words "ANGLO SAXON" on it in large gilt letters, as if it were a useless part which the ship could afford to lose, or which the sailors had discharged at the same time with the pilot. But it interested somewhat as if it had been a part of the Argo, clipped off in passing through the Symplegades.

To the fisherman, the Cape itself is a sort of store-ship laden with supplies,—a safer and larger craft which carries the women and children, the old men and the sick; and indeed sea-phrases are as common on it as on board a vessel. Thus is it ever with a sea-going people. The old Northmen used to speak of the "keel-ridge" of the country, that is, the ridge of the Doffrafield Mountains, as if the land were a boat turned bottom up. I was frequently reminded of the Northmen here. The inhabitants of the Cape are often at once farmers and sea-rovers; they are more than vikings or kings of the bays, for their sway extends over the open sea also. A farmer in Wellfleet, at whose house I afterward spent a night, who had raised fifty bushels of potatoes the previous year, which is a large crop for the Cape, and had extensive salt-works, pointed to his schooner, which lay in sight, in which he and his man and boy occasionally ran down the coast a-trading as far as the Capes of Virginia. This was his market-cart, and his hired man knew how to steer her. Thus he drove two teams a-field,

> "ere the high *seas* appeared
> Under the opening eyelids of the morn."

Though probably he would not hear much of the "gray fly" on his way to Virginia.

A great proportion of the inhabitants of the Cape are always thus abroad about their teaming on some ocean highway or other, and the history of one of their ordinary trips would cast the Argonautic expedition into the shade. I have just heard of a Cape Cod captain who was expected home in the beginning of the winter from the West Indies, but was long since given up for lost, till his relations at length have heard with joy, that, after getting within forty miles of Cape Cod light, he was driven back by nine successive gales to Key West, between Florida and Cuba, and was once again shaping his course for home. Thus he spent his winter. In ancient times the adventures of these two or three men and boys would have been made the basis of a myth, but now such tales are crowded into a line of shorthand signs, like an algebraic formula in the shipping news. "Wherever over the world," said Palfrey in his oration at Barnstable, "you see the stars and stripes floating, you may have good hope that beneath them some one will be found who can tell you the soundings of Barnstable, or Wellfleet, or Chatham Harbor."

I passed by the home of somebody's (or everybody's) Uncle Bill, one day over on the Plymouth shore. It was a schooner half keeled-up on the mud: we aroused the master out of a sound sleep at noonday, by thumping on the bottom of his vessel till he presented himself at the hatchway, for we wanted to borrow his clam-digger. Meaning to make him a call, I looked out the next morning, and lo! he had run over to "the Pines" the evening before, fearing an easterly storm. He outrode the *great* gale in the spring of 1851, dashing about alone in Plymouth Bay. He goes after rockweed, lighters vessels, and saves wrecks. I still saw him lying in the mud over at "the Pines" in the horizon, which place he could not leave if he would till flood tide. But he would not then probably. This waiting for the tide is a singular feature in life by the sea-shore. A frequent answer is, "Well! you can't start for two hours yet." It is something new to a landsman, and at first he is not disposed to wait. History says that "two inhabitants of Truro were the first who adventured to the Falkland Isles in pursuit of whales. This voyage was undertaken in the year 1774, by the advice of Admiral Montague of the British navy, and was crowned with success."

At the Pond Village we saw a pond three eighths of a mile long densely filled with cat-tail flags, seven feet high,—enough for all the coopers in New England.

Pond Village

The western shore was nearly as sandy as the eastern, but the water was much smoother, and the bottom was partially covered with the slender grass-like seaweed (*Zostera*), which we had not seen on the Atlantic side; there were also a few rude sheds for trying fish on the beach there, which made it appear less wild. In the few marshes on this side we afterward saw Samphire, Rosemary, and other plants new to us inlanders.

In the summer and fall sometimes, hundreds of blackfish (the Social Whale, *Globicephalus Melas* of De Kay; called also Black Whale-fish, Howling Whale, Bottlehead, etc.), fifteen feet or more in length, are driven ashore in a single school here. I witnessed such a scene in July, 1855. A carpenter who was working at the lighthouse arriving early in the morning remarked that he did not know but he had lost fifty dollars by coming to his work; for as he came along the Bay side he heard them driving a school of blackfish ashore, and he had debated with himself whether he should not go and join them and take his share, but had concluded to come to his work. After breakfast I came over to this place, about two miles distant, and near the beach met some of the fishermen returning from their chase. Looking up and down the shore, I could see about a mile south some large black masses on the sand, which I knew must be blackfish, and a man or two about them. As I walked along towards them I soon came to a huge carcass whose head was gone and whose blubber had been stripped off some weeks before; the tide was just beginning to move it, and the stench compelled me to go a long way round. When I came to Great Hollow I found a fisherman and some boys on the watch, and counted about thirty blackfish, just killed, with many lance wounds, and the water was more or less bloody around. They were partly on shore and partly in the water, held by a rope round their tails till the tide should leave them. A boat had been somewhat stove by the tail of one. They were a smooth shining black, like India-rubber, and had remarkably simple and lumpish forms for animated creatures, with a blunt round snout or head, whale-like, and simple stiff-looking flippers. The largest were about fifteen feet long, but one or two were only five feet long, and still without teeth. The fisherman slashed one with his jackknife, to show me how thick the blubber was,—about three inches; and as I passed my finger through the cut it was covered thick with oil. The blubber looked like pork, and this man said that when they were trying it the boys would sometimes come round with a piece of bread in one hand, and take a piece of blubber in the other to eat with it, preferring it to pork scraps. He also cut into the flesh beneath, which was firm and red like beef, and he said that for his part he preferred it when fresh to beef. It is stated that in 1812 blackfish were used as food by the poor of Bretagne. They were waiting for the tide to leave these fishes high and dry, that they might strip off the blubber and carry it to their try-works in their boats, where they try it on the beach. They get commonly a barrel of oil, worth fifteen or twenty dollars, to a fish. There were many lances and harpoons in the boats,—much slenderer instruments than I had expected. An old man came along the beach with a horse and wagon distributing the dinners of the fishermen, which their wives had put up in little pails and jugs, and which he had collected in the Pond Village, and for this service, I suppose, he received a share of the oil. If one could not tell his own pail, he took the first he came to.

As I stood there they raised the cry of "another school," and we could see their black backs and their blowing about a mile northward, as they went leaping over the sea like horses. Some boats were already in pursuit there, driving them toward the beach. Other fishermen and boys running up began to jump into the boats and push them off from where I stood, and I might have gone too had I chosen. Soon there were twenty-five or thirty boats in pursuit, some large ones under sail, and others rowing with might and main, keeping outside of the school, those nearest to the fishes striking on the sides of their boats and blowing horns to drive them on to the beach. It was an exciting race. If they succeed in driving them ashore each boat takes one share, and then each man, but if they are compelled to strike them off shore each boat's company take what they strike. I walked rapidly along the shore toward the north, while the fishermen were rowing still more swiftly to join their companions, and a little boy who walked by my side was congratulating himself that his father's boat was beating another one. An old blind fisherman whom we met, inquired, "Where are they? I can't see. Have they got them?" In the mean while the fishes had turned and were escaping northward toward Provincetown, only occasionally the back of one being seen. So the nearest crews were compelled to strike them, and we saw several boats soon made fast, each to its fish, which, four or five rods ahead, was drawing it like a race-horse straight toward the beach, leaping half out of water, blowing blood and water from its hole, and leaving a streak of foam behind. But they went ashore too far north for us, though we could see the fishermen leap out and lance them on the sand. It was just like pictures of whaling which I have seen, and a fisherman told me that it was nearly as dangerous. In his first trial he had been much excited, and in his haste had used a lance with its scabbard on, but nevertheless had thrust it quite through his fish.

I learned that a few days before this one hundred and eighty blackfish had been driven ashore in one school at Eastham, a little farther south, and that the keeper of Billingsgate Point light went out one morning about the same time and cut his initials on the backs of a large school which had run ashore in the night, and sold his right to them to Provincetown for one thousand dollars, and probably Provincetown made as much more. Another fisherman told me that nineteen years ago three hundred and eighty were driven ashore in one school at Great Hollow. In the Naturalists' Library, it is said that, in the winter of 1809-10, one thousand one hundred and ten "approached the shore of Hralfiord, Iceland, and were captured." De Kay says it is not known why they are stranded. But one fisherman declared to me that they ran ashore in pursuit of squid, and that they generally came on the coast about the last of July.

About a week afterward, when I came to this shore, it was strewn, as far as I could see with a glass, with the carcasses of blackfish stripped of their blubber and their heads cut off; the latter lying higher up. Walking on the beach was out of the question on account of the stench. Between Provincetown and Truro they lay in the very path of the stage. Yet no steps were taken to abate the nuisance, and men were catching lobsters as usual just off the shore. I was told that they did sometimes tow them out and sink them; yet I wondered where they got the stones to sink them with. Of course they might be made into guano, and Cape Cod is not so fertile that her inhabitants can afford to do without this manure,—to say nothing of the diseases they may produce.

After my return home, wishing to learn what was known about the Blackfish, I had recourse to the reports of the zoological surveys of the State, and I found that Storer had rightfully omitted it in his Report on the Fishes, since it is not a fish; so I turned to Emmons's Report of the Mammalia, but was surprised to find that the seals and whales were omitted by him, because he had had no opportunity to observe them. Considering how this State has risen and thriven by its fisheries.—that the legislature which authorized the Zoological Survey sat under the emblem of a codfish,—that Nantucket and New Bedford are within our limits,—that an early riser may find a thousand or fifteen hundred dollars' worth of blackfish on the shore in a morning,—that the Pilgrims saw the Indians cutting up a blackfish on the shore at

Eastham, and called a part of that shore "Grampus Bay," from the number of blackfish they found there, before they got to Plymouth,— and that from that time to this these fishes have continued to enrich one or two counties almost annually, and that their decaying carcasses were now poisoning the air of one county for more than thirty miles,— I thought it remarkable that neither the popular nor scientific name was to be found in a report on our mammalia,—a catalogue of the productions of our land and water.

We had here, as well as all across the Cape, a fair view of Provincetown, five or six miles distant over the water toward the west, under its shrubby sand-hills, with its harbor now full of vessels whose masts mingled with the spires of its churches, and gave it the appearance of a quite large seaport town.

The inhabitants of all the lower Cape towns enjoy thus the prospect of two seas. Standing on the western or larboard shore, and looking across to where the distant mainland looms, they can say. This is Massachusetts Bay; and then, after an hour's sauntering walk, they may stand on the starboard side, beyond which no land is seen to loom, and say, This is the Atlantic Ocean.

On our way back to the lighthouse, by whose white-washed tower we steered as securely as the mariner by its light at night, we passed through a graveyard, which apparently was saved from being blown away by its slates, for they had enabled a thick bed of huckleberry-bushes to root themselves amid the graves. We thought it would be worth the while to read the epitaphs where so many were lost at sea; however, as not only their lives, but commonly their bodies also, were lost or not identified, there were fewer epitaphs of this sort than we expected, though there were not a few. Their graveyard is the ocean. Near the eastern side we started up a fox in a hollow, the only kind of wild quadruped, if I except a skunk in a salt-marsh, that we saw in all our walk (unless painted and box tortoises may be called quadrupeds). He was a large, plump, shaggy fellow, like a yellow dog, with, as usual, a white tip to his tail, and looked as if he fared well on the Cape. He cantered away into the shrub-oaks and bayberry-bushes which chanced to grow there, but were hardly high enough to conceal him. I saw another the next summer leaping over the top of a beach-plum a little farther north, a small arc of his course (which I trust is not yet run), from which I endeavored in vain to calculate his whole orbit: there were too many unknown attractions to be allowed for. I also saw the exuviae of a third fast sinking into the sand, and added the skull to my collection. Hence I concluded that they must be plenty thereabouts; but a traveller may meet with more than an inhabitant, since he is more likely to take an unfrequented route across the country. They told me that in some years they died off in great numbers by a kind of madness, under the effect of which they were seen whirling round and round as if in pursuit of their tails. In Crantz's account of Greenland, he says: "They (the foxes) live upon birds and their eggs, and, when they can't get them, upon crowberries, mussels, crabs, and what the sea casts out."

Just before reaching the light-house, we saw the sun set in the Bay,—for standing on that narrow Cape was, as I have said, like being on the deck of a vessel, or rather at the masthead of a man-of-war, thirty miles at sea, though we knew that at the same moment the sun was setting behind our native hills, which were just below the horizon in that direction. This sight drove everything else quite out of our heads, and Homer and the Ocean came in again with a rush,—

Ἐν δ' ἔπεσ' Ὠκεανῷ λαμπρὸν φάος ἠελίοιο,

the shining torch of the sun fell into the ocean.

## VIII

## THE HIGHLAND LIGHT

This light-house, known to mariners as the Cape Cod or Highland Light, is one of our "primary sea-coast lights," and is usually the first seen by those approaching the entrance of Massachusetts Bay from Europe. It is forty-three miles from Cape Ann Light, and forty-one from Boston Light. It stands about twenty rods from the edge of the bank, which is here formed of clay. I borrowed the plane and square, level and dividers, of a carpenter who was shingling a barn near by, and using one of those shingles made of a mast, contrived a rude sort of quadrant, with pins for sights and pivots, and got the angle of elevation of the Bank opposite the light-house, and with a couple of cod-lines the length of its slope, and so measured its height on the shingle. It rises one hundred and ten feet above its immediate base, or about one hundred and twenty-three feet above mean low water. Graham, who has carefully surveyed the extremity of the Cape, makes it one hundred and thirty feet. The mixed sand and clay lay at an angle of forty degrees with the horizon, where I measured it, but the clay is generally much steeper. No cow nor hen ever gets down it. Half a mile farther south the bank is fifteen or twenty-five feet higher, and that appeared to be the highest land in North Truro. Even this vast clay bank is fast wearing away. Small streams of water trickling down it at intervals of two or three rods, have left the intermediate clay in the form of steep Gothic roofs fifty feet high or more, the ridges as sharp and rugged-looking as rocks; and in one place the bank is curiously eaten out in the form of a large semicircular crater.

Dragging a dory up on the beach

According to the light-house keeper, the Cape is wasting here on both sides, though most on the eastern. In some places it had lost many rods within the last year, and, erelong, the light-house must be moved. We calculated, *from his data*, how soon the Cape would be quite worn away at this point, "for," said he, "I can remember sixty years back." We were even more surprised at this last announcement,—that is, at the slow waste of life and energy in our informant, for we had taken him to be not more than forty,—than at the rapid wasting of the Cape, and we thought that he stood a fair chance to outlive the former.

Between this October and June of the next year I found that the bank had lost about forty feet in one place, opposite the light-house, and it was cracked more than forty feet farther from the edge at the last date, the shore being strewn with the recent rubbish. But I judged that generally it was not wearing away here at the rate of more than six feet annually. Any conclusions drawn from the observations of a few years or one generation only are likely to prove false, and the Cape may balk expectation by its durability. In some places even a wrecker's foot-path down the bank lasts several years. One old inhabitant told us that when the light-house was built, in 1798, it was calculated that it would stand forty-five years, allowing the bank to waste one length of fence each year, "but," said he, "there it is" (or rather another near the same site, about twenty rods from the edge of the bank).

The sea is not gaining on the Cape everywhere, for one man told me of a vessel wrecked long ago on the north of Provincetown whose "bones" (this was his word) are still visible many rods within the present line of the beach, half buried in sand. Perchance they lie alongside the timbers of a whale. The general statement of the inhabitants is that the Cape is wasting on both sides, but extending itself on particular points on the south and west, as at Chatham and Monomoy Beaches, and at Billingsgate, Long, and Race Points. James Freeman stated in his day that above three miles had been added to Monomoy Beach during the previous fifty years, and it is said to be still extending as fast as ever. A writer in the Massachusetts Magazine, in the last century, tells us that "when the English first settled upon the Cape, there was an island off Chatham, at three leagues' distance, called Webbs' Island, containing twenty acres, covered with red-cedar or savin. The inhabitants of Nantucket used to carry wood from it"; but he adds that in his day a large rock alone marked the spot, and the water was six fathoms deep there. The entrance to Nauset Harbor, which was once in Eastham, has now travelled south into Orleans. The islands in Wellfleet Harbor once formed a continuous beach, though now small vessels pass between them. And so of many other parts of this coast.

Perhaps what the Ocean takes from one part of the Cape it gives to another,—robs Peter to pay Paul. On the eastern side the sea appears to be everywhere encroaching on the land. Not only the land is undermined, and its ruins carried off by currents, but the sand is blown from the beach directly up the steep bank where it is one hundred and fifty feet high, and covers the original surface there many feet deep. If you sit on the edge you will have ocular demonstration of this by soon getting your eyes full. Thus the bank preserves its height as fast as it is worn away. This sand is steadily travelling westward at a rapid rate, "more than a hundred yards," says one writer, within the memory of inhabitants now living; so that in some places peat-meadows are buried deep under the sand, and the peat is cut through it; and in one place a large peat-meadow has made its appearance on the shore in the bank covered many feet deep, and peat has been cut there. This accounts for that great pebble of peat which we saw in the surf. The old oysterman had told us that many years ago he lost a "crittur" by her being mired in a swamp near the Atlantic side east of his house, and twenty years ago he lost the swamp itself entirely, but has since seen signs of it appearing on the beach. He also said that he had seen cedar stumps "as big as cart-wheels"(!) on the bottom of the Bay, three miles off Billingsate Point, when leaning over the side of his boat in pleasant weather, and that that was dry land not long ago. Another told us that a log canoe known to have been buried many years before on the Bay side at East Harbor in Truro, where the Cape is extremely narrow, appeared at length on the Atlantic side, the Cape having rolled over it, and an old woman said,—"Now, you see, it is true what I told you, that the Cape is moving."

The bars along the coast shift with every storm, and in many places there is occasionally none at all. We ourselves observed the effect of a single storm with a high tide in the night, in July, 1855. It moved the sand on the beach opposite the light-house to the depth of six feet, and three rods in width as far as we could see north and south, and carried it bodily off no one knows exactly where, laying bare in one place a large rock five feet high which was invisible before, and narrowing the beach to that extent. There is usually, as I have said, no bathing on the back-side of the Cape, on account of the undertow, but when we were there last, the sea had, three months before, cast up a bar near this lighthouse, two miles long and ten rods wide, over which the tide did not flow, leaving a narrow cove, then a quarter of a mile long, between it and the shore, which afforded excellent bathing. This cove had from time to time been closed up as the bar travelled northward, in one instance imprisoning four or five hundred whiting and cod, which died there, and the water as often turned fresh, and finally gave place to sand. This bar, the inhabitants assured us, might be wholly removed, and the water six feet deep there in two or three days.

The light-house keeper said that when the wind blowed strong on to the shore, the waves ate fast into the bank, but when it blowed off they took no sand away; for in the former case the wind heaped up the surface of the water next to the beach, and to preserve its equilibrium a strong undertow immediately set back again into the sea which carried with it the sand and whatever else was in the way, and left the beach hard to walk on; but in the latter case the undertow set on and carried the sand with it, so that it was particularly difficult for shipwrecked men to get to land when the wind blowed on to the shore, but easier when it blowed off. This undertow, meeting the next surface wave on the bar which itself has made, forms part of the dam over which the latter breaks, as over an upright wall. The sea thus plays with the land holding a sand-bar in its mouth awhile before it swallows it, as a cat plays with a mouse; but the fatal gripe is sure to come at last. The sea sends its rapacious east wind to rob the land, but before the former has got far with its prey, the land sends its honest west wind to recover some of its own. But, according to Lieutenant Davis, the forms, extent, and distribution of sand-bars and banks are principally determined, not by winds and waves but by tides.

Our host said that you would be surprised if you were on the beach when the wind blew a hurricane directly on to it, to see that none of the drift-wood came ashore, but all was carried directly northward and parallel with the shore as fast as a man can walk, by the inshore current, which sets strongly in that direction at flood tide. The strongest swimmers also are carried along with it, and never gain an inch toward the beach. Even a large rock has been moved half a mile northward along-the beach. He assured us that the sea was never still on the backside of the Cape, but ran commonly as high as your head, so that a great part of the time you could not launch a boat there, and even in the calmest weather the waves run six or eight feet up the beach, though then you could get off on a plank. Champlain and Pourtrincourt could not land here in 1606, on account of the swell (*la houlle*), yet the savages came off to them in a canoe. In the Sieur de la Borde's "Relation des Caraibes," my edition of which was published at Amsterdam in 1711, at page 530 he says:—

"Couroumon a Caraibe, also a star [*i.e.* a god], makes the great *lames à la mer*, and overturns canoes. *Lames à la mer* are the long *vagues* which are not broken (*entrecoupées*), and such as one sees come to land all in one piece, from one end of a beach to another, so that, however little wind there may be, a shallop or a canoe could hardly land (*aborder terre*) without turning over, or being filled with water."

But on the Bay side the water even at its edge is often as smooth and still as in a pond. Commonly there are no boats used along this beach. There was a boat belonging to the Highland Light which the next keeper after he had been there a year had not launched, though he said that there was good fishing just off the shore. Generally the Life Boats cannot be used when needed. When the waves run very high it is impossible to get a boat off, however skilfully you steer it, for it will often be completely covered by the curving edge of the approaching breaker as by an arch, and so filled with water, or it will be lifted up by its bows, turned directly over backwards, and all the contents spilled out. A spar thirty feet long is served in the same way.

I heard of a party who went off fishing back of Wellfleet some years ago, in two boats, in calm weather, who, when they had laden their boats with fish, and approached the land again, found such a swell breaking on it, though there was no wind, that they were afraid to enter it. At first they thought to pull for Provincetown, but night was coming on, and that was many miles distant. Their case seemed a desperate one. As often as they approached the shore and saw the terrible breakers that intervened, they were deterred. In short, they were thoroughly frightened. Finally, having thrown their fish overboard, those in one boat chose a favorable opportunity, and succeeded, by skill and good luck, in reaching the land, but they were unwilling to take the responsibility of telling the others when to come in, and as the other helmsman was inexperienced, their boat was swamped at once, yet all managed to save themselves.

Much smaller waves soon make a boat "nail-sick," as the phrase is. The keeper said that after a long and strong blow there would be three large waves, each successively larger than the last, and then no large ones for some time, and that, when they wished to land in a boat, they came in on the last and largest wave. Sir Thomas Browne (as quoted in Brand's Popular Antiquities, p. 372), on the subject of the tenth wave being "greater or more dangerous than any other," after quoting Ovid,—

    "Qui venit hic fluctus, fluctus supereminet omnes
    Posterior nono est, undecimo que prior,"—

says, "Which, notwithstanding, is evidently false; nor can it be made out either by observation either upon the shore or the ocean, as we have with diligence explored in both. And surely in vain we expect regularity in the waves of the sea, or in the particular motions thereof, as we may in its general reciprocations, whose causes are constant, and effects therefore correspondent; whereas its fluctuations are but motions subservient, which winds, storms, shores, shelves, and every interjacency, irregulates."

We read that the Clay Pounds, were so called "because vessels have had the misfortune to be pounded against it in gales of wind," which we regard as a doubtful derivation. There are small ponds here, upheld by the clay, which were formerly called the Clay Pits. Perhaps this, or Clay Ponds, is the origin of the name. Water is found in the clay quite near the surface; but we heard of one man who had sunk a well in the sand close by, "till he could see stars at noonday," without finding any. Over this bare Highland the wind has full sweep. Even in July it blows the wings over the heads of the young turkeys, which do not know enough to head against it; and in gales the doors and windows are blown in, and you must hold on to the lighthouse to prevent being blown into the Atlantic. They who merely keep out on the beach in a storm in the winter are sometimes rewarded by the Humane Society. If you would feel the full force of a tempest, take up your residence on the top of Mount Washington, or at the Highland Light, in Truro.

It was said in 1794 that more vessels were cast away on the east shore of Truro than anywhere in Barnstable County. Notwithstanding that this light-house has since been erected, after almost every storm we read of one or more vessels wrecked here, and sometimes more than a dozen wrecks are visible from this point at one time. The inhabitants hear the crash of vessels going to pieces as they sit round their hearths, and they commonly date from some memorable shipwreck. If the history of this beach could be written from beginning to end, it would be a thrilling page in the history of commerce.

Truro was settled in the year 1700 as *Dangerfield*. This was a very appropriate name, for I afterward read on a monument in the graveyard, near Pamet River, the following inscription:—

<blockquote>
Sacred<br>
to the memory of<br>
57 citizens of Truro,<br>
who were lost in seven<br>
vessels, which<br>
foundered at sea in<br>
the memorable gale<br>
of Oct. 3d, 1841.
</blockquote>

Their names and ages by families were recorded on different sides of the stone. They are said to have been lost on George's Bank, and I was told that only one vessel drifted ashore on the backside of the Cape, with the boys locked into the cabin and drowned. It is said that the homes of all were "within a circuit of two miles." Twenty-eight inhabitants of Dennis were lost in the same gale; and I read that "in one day, immediately after this storm, nearly or quite one hundred bodies were taken up and buried on Cape Cod." The Truro Insurance Company failed for want of skippers to take charge of its vessels. But the surviving inhabitants went a-fishing again the next year as usual. I found that it would not do to speak of shipwrecks there, for almost every family has lost some of its members at sea. "Who lives in that house?" I inquired. "Three widows," was the reply. The stranger and the inhabitant view the shore with very different eyes. The former may have come to see and admire the ocean in a storm; but the latter looks on it as the scene where his nearest relatives were wrecked. When I remarked to an old wrecker partially blind, who was sitting on the edge of the bank smoking a pipe, which he had just lit with a match of dried beach-grass, that I supposed he liked to hear the sound of the surf, he answered: "No, I do not like to hear the sound of the surf." He had lost at least one son in "the memorable gale," and could tell many a tale of the shipwrecks which he had witnessed there.

In the year 1717, a noted pirate named Bellamy was led on to the bar off Wellfleet by the captain of a *snow* which he had taken, to whom he had offered his vessel again if he would pilot him into Provincetown Harbor. Tradition says that the latter threw over a burning tar-barrel in the night, which drifted ashore, and the pirates followed it. A storm coming on, their whole fleet was wrecked, and more than a hundred dead bodies lay along the shore. Six who escaped shipwreck were executed. "At times to this day" (1793), says the historian of Wellfleet, "there are King William and Queen Mary's coppers picked up, and pieces of silver called cob-money. The violence of the seas moves the sands on the outer bar, so that at times the iron caboose of the ship [that is, Bellamy's] at low ebbs has been seen." Another tells us that, "For many years after this shipwreck, a man of a very singular and frightful aspect used every spring and autumn to be seen travelling on the Cape, who was supposed to have been one of Bellamy's crew. The presumption is that he went to some place where money had been secreted by the pirates, to get such a supply as his exigencies required. When he died, many pieces of gold were found in a girdle which he constantly wore."

An old wrecker at home

As I was walking on the beach here in my last visit, looking for shells and pebbles, just after that storm, which I have mentioned as moving the sand to a great depth, not knowing but I might find some cob-money, I did actually pick up a French crown piece, worth about a dollar and six cents, near high-water mark, on the still moist sand, just under the abrupt, caving base of the bank. It was of a dark slate color, and looked like a flat pebble, but still bore a very distinct and handsome head of Louis XV., and the usual legend on the reverse. *Sit*

*Nomen Domini Benedictum* (Blessed be the Name of the Lord), a pleasing sentiment to read in the sands of the sea-shore, whatever it might be stamped on, and I also made out the date, 1741. Of course, I thought at first that it was that same old button which I have found so many times, but my knife soon showed the silver. Afterward, rambling on the bars at low tide, I cheated my companion by holding up round shells (*Scutellæ*) between my fingers, whereupon he quickly stripped and came off to me.

In the Revolution, a British ship of war called the Somerset was wrecked near the Clay Pounds, and all on board, some hundreds in number, were taken prisoners. My informant said that he had never seen any mention of this in the histories, but that at any rate he knew of a silver watch, which one of those prisoners by accident left there, which was still going to tell the story. But this event is noticed by some writers.

The next summer I saw a sloop from Chatham dragging for anchors and chains just oft' this shore. She had her boats out at the work while she shuffled about on various tacks, and, when anything was found, drew up to hoist it on board. It is a singular employment, at which men are regularly hired and paid for their industry, to hunt to-day in pleasant weather for anchors which have been lost,—the sunken faith and hope of mariners, to which they trusted in vain; now, perchance, it is the rusty one of some old pirate's ship or Norman fisherman, whose cable parted here two hundred years ago; and now the best bower anchor of a Canton or a California ship, which has gone about her business. If the roadsteads of the spiritual ocean could be thus dragged, what rusty flukes of hope deceived and parted chain-cables of faith might again be windlassed aboard! enough to sink the finder's craft, or stock new navies to the end of time. The bottom of the sea is strewn with anchors, some deeper and some shallower, and alternately covered and uncovered by the sand, perchance with a small length of iron cable still attached,—to which where is the other end? So many unconcluded tales to be continued another time. So, if we had diving-bells adapted to the spiritual deeps, we should see anchors with their cables attached, as thick as eels in vinegar, all wriggling vainly toward their holding-ground. But that is not treasure for us which another man has lost; rather it is for us to seek what no other man has found or can find,— not be Chatham men, dragging for anchors.

The annals of this voracious beach! who could write them, unless it were a shipwrecked sailor? How many who have seen it have seen it only in the midst of danger and distress, the last strip of earth which their mortal eyes beheld. Think of the amount of suffering which a single strand has witnessed. The ancients would have represented it as a sea-monster with open jaws, more terrible than Scylla and Charybdis. An inhabitant of Truro told me that about a fortnight after the *St. John* was wrecked at Cohasset he found two bodies on the shore at the Clay Pounds. They were those of a man, and a corpulent woman. The man had thick boots on, though his head was off, but "it was alongside." It took the finder some weeks to get over the sight. Perhaps they were man and wife, and whom God had joined the ocean currents had not put asunder. Yet by what slight accidents at first may they have been associated in their drifting. Some of the bodies of those passengers were picked up far out at sea, boxed up and sunk; some brought ashore and buried. There are more consequences to a shipwreck than the underwriters notice. The Gulf Stream may return some to their native shores, or drop them in some out-of-the-way cave of Ocean, where time and the elements will write new riddles with their bones.—But to return to land again.

In this bank, above the clay, I counted in the summer, two hundred holes of the Bank Swallow within a space six rods long, and there were at least one thousand old birds within three times that distance, twittering over the surf. I had never associated them in my thoughts with the beach before. One little boy who had been a-birds-nesting had got eighty swallows' eggs for his share! Tell it not to the Humane Society. There were many young birds on the clay beneath, which had tumbled out and died. Also there were many Crow-blackbirds hopping about in the dry fields, and the Upland Plover were breeding close by the light-house. The keeper had once cut off one's wing while mowing, as she sat on her eggs there. This is also a favorite resort for gunners in the fall to shoot the Golden Plover. As around the shores of a pond are seen devil's-needles, butterflies, etc., so here, to my surprise, I saw at the same season great devil's-needles of a size proportionably larger, or nearly as big as my finger, incessantly coasting up and down the edge of the bank, and butterflies also were hovering over it, and I never saw so many dorr-bugs and beetles of various kinds as strewed the beach. They had apparently flown over the bank in the night, and could not get up again, and some had perhaps fallen into the sea and were washed ashore. They may have been in part attracted by the light-house lamps.

The Clay Pounds are a more fertile tract than usual. We saw some fine patches of roots and corn here. As generally on the Cape, the plants had little stalk or leaf, but ran remarkably to seed. The corn was hardly more than half as high as in the interior, yet the ears were large and full, and one farmer told us that he could raise forty bushels on an acre without manure, and sixty with it. The heads of the rye also were remarkably large. The Shadbush (*Amelanchier*), Beach Plums, and Blueberries (*Vaccinium Pennsylvanicum*), like the apple-trees and oaks, were very dwarfish, spreading over the sand, but at the same time very fruitful. The blueberry was but an inch or two high, and its fruit often rested on the ground, so that you did not suspect the presence of the bushes, even on those bare hills, until you were treading on them. I thought that this fertility must be owing mainly to the abundance of moisture in the atmosphere, for I observed that what little grass there was was remarkably laden with dew in the morning, and in summer dense imprisoning fogs frequently last till midday, turning one's beard into a wet napkin about his throat, and the oldest inhabitant may lose his way within a stone's throw of his house or be obliged to follow the beach for a guide. The brick house attached to the light-house was exceedingly damp at that season, and, writing-paper lost all its stiffness in it. It was impossible to dry your towel after bathing, or to press flowers without their mildewing. The air was so moist that we rarely wished to drink, though we could at all times taste the salt on our lips. Salt was rarely used at table, and our host told us that his cattle invariably refused it when it was offered them, they got so much with their grass and at every breath, but he said that a sick horse or one just from the country would sometimes take a hearty draught of salt water, and seemed to like it and be the better for it.

It was surprising to see how much water was contained in the terminal bud of the sea-side golden-rod, standing in the sand early in July, and also how turnips, beets, carrots, etc., flourished even in pure sand. A man travelling by the shore near there not long before us noticed something green growing in the pure sand of the beach, just at high-water mark, and on approaching found it to be a bed of beets flourishing vigorously, probably from seed washed out of the *Franklin*. Also beets and turnips came up in the sea-weed used for manure in many parts of the Cape. This suggests how various plants may have been dispersed over the world to distant islands and continents. Vessels, with seeds in their cargoes, destined for particular ports, where perhaps they were not needed, have been cast away on desolate islands, and though their crews perished, some of their seeds have been preserved. Out of many kinds a few would find a soil and climate adapted to them, become naturalized, and perhaps drive out the native plants at last, and so fit the land for the habitation of man. It is an ill wind that blows nobody any good, and for the time lamentable shipwrecks may thus contribute a new vegetable to a continent's stock, and prove on the whole a lasting blessing to its inhabitants. Or winds and currents might effect the same without the intervention of man. What indeed are the various succulent plants which grow on the beach but such beds of beets and turnips, sprung originally from seeds which perhaps were cast on the waters for this end, though we do not know the *Franklin* which they came out of? In ancient times some Mr. Bell (?) was sailing this way in his ark with seeds of rocket, salt-wort, sandwort, beachgrass, samphire, bayberry, poverty-grass, etc., all nicely labelled with directions, intending to establish a nursery somewhere; and did not a nursery get established, though he thought that he had failed?

About the light-house I observed in the summer the pretty *Polygala polygama*, spreading ray-wise flat on the ground, white pasture thistles (*Cirsium pumilum*), and amid the shrubbery the *Smilax glauca*, which is commonly said not to grow so far north; near the edge of the banks about half a mile southward, the broom crow-berry (*Empetrum*

*Conradii*), for which Plymouth is the only locality in Massachusetts usually named, forms pretty green mounds four or five feet in diameter by one foot high,—soft, springy beds for the wayfarer. I saw it afterward in Provincetown, but prettiest of all the scarlet pimpernel, or poor-man's weather-glass (*Anagallis-arvensis*), greets you in fair weather on almost every square yard of sand. From Yarmouth, I have received the *Chrysopsis falcata* (golden aster), and *Vaccinium stamineum* (Deerberry or Squaw Huckleberry), with fruit not edible, sometimes as large as a cranberry (Sept. 7).

The Highland Light

The Highland Light-house,[1] where we were staying, is a substantial-looking building of brick, painted white, and surmounted by an iron cap. Attached to it is the dwelling of the keeper, one story high, also of brick, and built by government. As we were going to spend the night in a light-house, we wished to make the most of so novel an experience, and therefore told our host that we would like to accompany him when he went to light up. At rather early candle-light he lighted a small Japan lamp, allowing it to smoke rather more than we like on ordinary occasions, and told us to follow him. He led the way first through his bedroom, which was placed nearest to the light-house, and then through a long, narrow, covered passage-way, between whitewashed walls like a prison entry, into the lower part of the light-house, where many great butts of oil were arranged around; thence we ascended by a winding and open iron stairway, with a steadily increasing scent of oil and lamp-smoke, to a trap-door in an iron floor, and through this into the lantern. It was a neat building, with everything in apple-pie order, and no danger of anything; rusting there for want of oil. The light consisted of fifteen argand lamps, placed within smooth concave reflectors twenty-one inches in diameter, and arranged in two horizontal circles one above the other, facing every way excepting directly down the Cape. These were surrounded, at a distance of two or three feet, by large plate-glass windows, which defied the storms, with iron sashes, on which rested the iron cap. All the iron work, except the floor, was painted white. And thus the light-house was completed. We walked slowly round in that narrow space as the keeper lighted each lamp in succession, conversing with him at the same moment that many a sailor on the deep witnessed the lighting of the Highland Light. His duty was to fill and trim and light his lamps, and keep bright the reflectors. He filled them every morning, and trimmed them commonly once in the course of the night. He complained of the quality of the oil which was furnished. This house consumes about eight hundred gallons in a year, which cost not far from one dollar a gallon; but perhaps a few lives would be saved if better oil were provided. Another light-house keeper said that the same proportion of winter-strained oil was sent to the southernmost light-house in the Union as to the most northern. Formerly, when this light-house had windows with small and thin panes, a severe storm would sometimes break the glass, and then they were obliged to put up a wooden shutter in haste to save their lights and reflectors,—and sometimes in tempests, when the mariner stood most in need of their guidance, they had thus nearly converted the light-house into a dark lantern, which emitted only a few feeble rays, and those commonly on the land or lee side. He spoke of the anxiety and sense of responsibility which he felt in cold and stormy nights in the winter; when he knew that many a poor fellow was depending on him, and his lamps burned dimly, the oil being chilled. Sometimes he was obliged to warm the oil in a kettle in his house at midnight, and fill his lamps over again,—for he could not have a fire in the light-house, it produced such a sweat on the windows. His successor told me that he could not keep too hot a fire in such a case. All this because the oil was poor. The government lighting the mariners on its wintry coast with summer-strained oil, to save expense! That were surely a summer-strained mercy.

This keeper's successor, who kindly entertained me the next year stated that one extremely cold night, when this and all the neighboring lights were burning summer oil, but he had been provident enough to reserve a little winter oil against emergencies, he was waked up with anxiety, and found that his oil was congealed, and his lights almost extinguished; and when, after many hours' exertion, he had succeeded in replenishing his reservoirs with winter oil at the wick end, and with difficulty had made them burn, he looked out and found that the other lights in the neighborhood, which were usually visible to him, had gone out, and he heard afterward that the Pamet River and Billingsgate Lights also had been extinguished.

Our host said that the frost, too, on the windows caused him much trouble, and in sultry summer nights the moths covered them and dimmed his lights; sometimes even small birds flew against the thick plate glass, and were found on the ground beneath in the morning with their necks broken. In the spring of 1855 he found nineteen small yellow-birds, perhaps goldfinches or myrtle-birds, thus lying dead around the light-house; and sometimes in the fall he had seen where a golden plover had struck the glass in the night, and left the down and the fatty part of its breast on it.

Thus he struggled, by every method, to keep his light shining before men. Surely the light-house keeper has a responsible, if an easy, office. When his lamp goes out, he goes out; or, at most, only one such accident is pardoned.

I thought it a pity that some poor student did not live there, to profit by all that light, since he would not rob the mariner. "Well," he said, "I do sometimes come up here and read the newspaper when they are noisy down below." Think of fifteen argand lamps to read the newspaper by! Government oil!—light, enough, perchance, to read the Constitution by! I thought that he should read nothing less than his Bible by that light. I had a classmate who fitted for college by the lamps of a light-house, which was more light, we think, than the University afforded.

When we had come down and walked a dozen rods from the light-house, we found that we could not get the full strength of its light on the narrow strip of land between it and the shore, being too low for the focus, and we saw only so many feeble and rayless stars; but at forty rods inland we could see to read, though we were still indebted to only one lamp. Each reflector sent forth a separate "fan" of light,—one shone on the windmill, and one in the hollow, while the intervening spaces were in shadow. This light is said to be visible twenty nautical miles and more from an observer fifteen feet above the level of the sea. We could see the revolving light at Race Point, the end of the Cape, about nine miles distant, and also the light on Long Point, at the entrance of Provincetown Harbor, and one of the distant Plymouth Harbor Lights, across the Bay, nearly in a range with the last, like a star in the horizon. The keeper thought that the other Plymouth Light was concealed by being exactly in a range with the Long Point Light. He told us that the mariner was sometimes led astray by a mackerel fisher's lantern, who was afraid of being run down in the night, or even by a cottager's light, mistaking them for some well-known light on the coast, and, when he discovered his mistake, was wont to curse the prudent fisher or the wakeful cottager without reason.

Though it was once declared that Providence placed this mass of clay here on purpose to erect a light-house on, the keeper said that the light-house should have been erected half a mile farther south, where the coast begins to bend, and where the light could be seen at the same time with the Nauset Lights, and distinguished from them. They now talk of building one there. It happens that the present one is the more useless now, so near the extremity of the Cape, because other light-houses have since been erected there.

Among the many regulations of the Light-house Board, hanging against the wall here, many of them excellent, perhaps, if there were a regiment stationed here to attend to them, there is one requiring the keeper to keep an account of the number of vessels which pass his light during the day. But there are a hundred vessels in sight at once, steering in all directions, many on the very verge of the horizon, and he must have more eyes than Argus, and be a good deal farther-sighted, to tell which are passing his light. It is an employment in some respects best suited to the habits of the gulls which coast up and down here, and circle over the sea.

I was told by the next keeper, that on the 8th of June following, a particularly clear and beautiful morning, he rose about half an hour before sunrise, and having a little time to spare, for his custom was to extinguish his lights at sunrise, walked down toward the shore to see what he might find. When he got to the edge of the bank he looked up, and, to his astonishment, saw the sun rising, and already part way above the horizon. Thinking that his clock was wrong, he made haste back, and though it was still too early by the clock, extinguished his lamps, and when he had got through and come down, he looked out the window, and, to his still greater astonishment, saw the sun just where it was before, two-thirds above the horizon. He showed me where its rays fell on the wall across the room. He proceeded to make a fire, and when he had done, there was the sun still at the same height. Whereupon, not trusting to his own eyes any longer, he called up his wife to look at it, and she saw it also. There were vessels in sight on the ocean, and their crews, too, he said, must have seen it, for its rays fell on them. It remained at that height for about fifteen minutes by the clock, and then rose as usual, and nothing else extraordinary happened during that day. Though accustomed to the coast, he had never witnessed nor heard of such a phenomenon before. I suggested that there might have been a cloud in the horizon invisible to him, which rose with the sun, and his clock was only as accurate as the average; or perhaps, as he denied the possibility of this, it was such a looming of the sun as is said to occur at Lake Superior and elsewhere. Sir John Franklin, for instance, says in his Narrative, that when he was on the shore of the Polar Sea, the horizontal refraction varied so much one morning that "the upper limb of the sun twice appeared at the horizon before it finally rose."

He certainly must be a son of Aurora to whom the sun looms, when there are so many millions to whom it *glooms* rather, or who never see it till an hour *after* it has risen. But it behooves us old stagers to keep our lamps trimmed and burning to the last, and not trust to the sun's looming.

This keeper remarked that the centre of the flame should be exactly opposite the centre of the reflectors, and that accordingly, if he was not careful to turn down his wicks in the morning, the sun falling on the reflectors on the south side of the building would set fire to them, like a burning-glass, in the coldest day, and he would look up at noon and see them all lighted! When your light is ready to give light, it is readiest to receive it, and the sun will light it. His successor said that he had never known them to blaze in such a case, but merely to smoke.

I saw that this was a place of wonders. In a sea turn or shallow fog while I was there the next summer, it being clear overhead, the edge of the bank twenty rods distant, appeared like a mountain pasture in the horizon. I was completely deceived by it, and I could then understand why mariners sometimes ran ashore in such cases, especially in the night, supposing it to be far away, though they could see the land. Once since this, being in a large oyster boat two or three hundred miles from here, in a dark night, when there was a thin veil of mist on land and water, we came so near to running on to the land before our skipper was aware of it, that the first warning was my hearing the sound of the surf under my elbow. I could almost have jumped ashore, and we were obliged to go about very suddenly to prevent striking. The distant light for which we were steering, supposing it a light-house five or six miles off, came through the cracks of a fisherman's bunk not more than six rods distant.

The keeper entertained us handsomely in his solitary little ocean house. He was a man of singular patience and intelligence, who, when our queries struck him, rung as clear as a bell in response. The light-house lamps a few feet distant shone full into my chamber, and made it as bright as day, so I knew exactly how the Highland Light bore all that night, and I was in no danger of being wrecked. Unlike the last, this was as still as a summer night. I thought, as I lay there, half awake and half asleep, looking upward through the window at the lights above my head, how many sleepless eyes from far out on the Ocean stream—mariners of all nations spinning their yarns through the various watches of the night—were directed toward my couch.

[1] The light-house has since been rebuilt, and shows a *Fresnel* light.

## IX

### THE SEA AND THE DESERT

The light-house lamps were still burning, though now with a silvery lustre, when I rose to see the sun come out of the Ocean; for he still rose eastward of us; but I was convinced that he must have come out of a dry bed beyond that stream, though he seemed to come out of the water.

> "The sun once more touched the fields,
> Mounting to heaven from the fair flowing
> Deep-running Ocean."

Now we saw countless sails of mackerel fishers abroad on the deep, one fleet in the north just pouring round the Cape, another standing down toward Chatham, and our host's son went off to join some lagging member of the first which had not yet left the Bay.

Before we left the light-house we were obliged to anoint our shoes faithfully with tallow, for walking on the beach, in the salt water and the sand, had turned them red and crisp. To counterbalance this, I have remarked that the seashore, even where muddy, as it is not here, is singularly clean; for notwithstanding the spattering of the water and mud and squirting of the clams while walking to and from the boat, your best black pants retain no stain nor dirt, such as they would acquire from walking in the country.

We have heard that a few days after this, when the Provincetown Bank was robbed, speedy emissaries from Provincetown made particular inquiries concerning us at this light-house. Indeed, they traced us all the way down the Cape, and concluded that we came by this unusual route down the back-side and on foot, in order that we might discover a way to get off with our booty when we had committed the robbery. The Cape is so long and narrow, and so bare withal, that it is wellnigh impossible for a stranger to visit it without the knowledge of its inhabitants generally, unless he is wrecked on to it in the night. So, when this robbery occurred, all their suspicions seem to have at once centred on us two travellers who had just passed down it. If we had not chanced to leave the Cape so soon, we should probably have been arrested. The real robbers were two young men from Worcester County who travelled with a centre-bit, and are said to have done their work very neatly. But the only bank that we pried into was the great Cape Cod sand-bank, and we robbed it only of an old French crown piece, some shells and pebbles, and the materials of this story.

Again we took to the beach for another day (October 13), walking along the shore of the resounding sea, determined to get it into us. We wished to associate with the Ocean until it lost the pond-like look which it wears to a country-man. We still thought that we could see the other side. Its surface was still more sparkling than the day before, and we beheld "the countless smilings of the ocean waves"; though some of them were pretty broad grins, for still the wind blew and the billows broke in foam along the beach. The nearest beach to us on the other side, whither we looked, due east, was on the coast of Galicia, in Spain, whose capital is Santiago, though by old poets' reckoning it should have been Atlantis or the Hesperides; but heaven is found to be farther west now. At first we were abreast of that part of Portugal *entre Douro e Mino*, and then Galicia and the port of Pontevedra opened to us as we walked along; but we did not enter, the breakers ran so high. The bold headland of Cape Finisterre, a little north of east, jutted toward us next, with its vain brag, for we flung back,—"Here is Cape Cod,—Cape Land's-Beginning." A little indentation toward the north,—for the land loomed to our imaginations by a common mirage,—we knew was the Bay of Biscay, and we sang:—

"There we lay, till next day.
  In the Bay of Biscay O!"

A little south of east was Palos, where Columbus weighed anchor, and farther yet the pillars which Hercules set up; concerning which when we inquired at the top of our voices what was written on them,—

for we had the morning sun in our faces, and could not see distinctly,—the inhabitants shouted *Ne plus ultra* (no more beyond), but the wind bore to us the truth only, *plus ultra* (more beyond), and over the Bay westward was echoed *ultra* (beyond). We spoke to them through the surf about the Far West, the true Hesperia, ἕω πέρας or end of the day, the This Side Sundown, where the sun was extinguished in the *Pacific*, and we advised them to pull up stakes and plant those pillars of theirs on the shore of California, whither all our folks were gone,—the only *ne* plus ultra now. Whereat they looked crestfallen on their cliffs, for we had taken the wind out of all their sails.

We could not perceive that any of their leavings washed up here, though we picked up a child's toy, a small dismantled boat, which may have been lost at Pontevedra.

The Cape became narrower and narrower as we approached its wrist between Truro and Provincetown, and the shore inclined more decidedly to the west. At the head of East Harbor Creek, the Atlantic is separated but by half a dozen rods of sand from the tide-waters of the Bay. From the Clay Pounds the bank flatted off for the last ten miles to the extremity at Race Point, though the highest parts, which are called "islands" from their appearance at a distance on the sea, were still seventy or eighty feet above the Atlantic, and afforded a good view of the latter, as well as a constant view of the Bay, there being no trees nor a hill sufficient to interrupt it. Also the sands began to invade the land more and more, until finally they had entire possession from sea to sea, at the narrowest part. For three or four miles between Truro and Provincetown there were no inhabitants from shore to shore, and there were but three or four houses for twice that distance.

As we plodded along, either by the edge of the ocean, where the sand was rapidly drinking up the last wave that wet it, or over the sand-hills of the bank, the mackerel fleet continued to pour round the Cape north of us, ten or fifteen miles distant, in countless numbers, schooner after schooner, till they made a city on the water. They were so thick that many appeared to be afoul of one another; now all standing on this tack, now on that. We saw how well the New-

Englanders had followed up Captain John Smith's suggestions with regard to the fisheries, made in 1616,—to what a pitch they had carried "this contemptible trade of fish," as he significantly styles it, and were now equal to the Hollanders whose example he holds up for the English to emulate; notwithstanding that "in this faculty," as he says, "the former are so naturalized, and of their vents so certainly acquainted, as there is no likelihood they will ever be paralleled, having two or three thousand busses, flat-bottoms, sword-pinks, todes, and such like, that breeds them sailors, mariners, soldiers, and merchants, never to be wrought out of that trade and fit for any other." We thought that it would take all these names and more to describe the numerous craft which we saw. Even then, some years before our "renowned sires" with their "peerless dames" stepped on Plymouth Rock, he wrote, "Newfoundland doth yearly freight neir eight hundred sail of ships with a silly, lean, skinny, poor-john, and cor fish," though all their supplies must be annually transported from Europe. Why not plant a colony here then, and raise those supplies on the spot? "Of all the four parts of the world," says he, "that I have yet seen, not inhabited, could I have but means to transport a colony, I would rather live here than anywhere. And if it did not maintain itself, were we but once indifferently well fitted, let us starve." Then "fishing before your doors," you "may every night sleep quietly ashore, with good cheer and what fires you will, or, when you please, with your wives and family." Already he anticipates "the new towns in New England in memory of their old,"—and who knows what may be discovered in the "heart and entrails" of the land, "seeing even the very edges," etc., etc.

Towing along shore

All this has been accomplished, and more, and where is Holland now? Verily the Dutch have taken it. There was no long interval between the suggestion of Smith and the eulogy of Burke.

Still one after another the mackerel schooners hove in sight round the head of the Cape, "whitening all the sea road," and we watched each one for a moment with an undivided interest. It seemed a pretty sport. Here in the country it is only a few idle boys or loafers that go a-fishing on a rainy day; but there it appeared as if every able-bodied man and helpful boy in the Bay had gone out on a pleasure excursion in their yachts, and all would at last land and have a chowder on the Cape.

The gazetteer tells you gravely how many of the men and boys of these towns are engaged in the whale, cod, and mackerel fishery, how many go to the banks of Newfoundland, or the coast of Labrador, the Straits of Belle Isle or the Bay of Chaleurs (Shalore the sailors call it); as if I were to reckon up the number of boys in Concord who are engaged during the summer in the perch, pickerel, bream, hornpout, and shiner fishery, of which no one keeps the statistics,—though I think that it is pursued with as much profit to the moral and intellectual man (or boy), and certainly with less danger to the physical one.

One of my playmates, who was apprenticed to a printer, and was somewhat of a wag, asked his master one afternoon if he might go a-fishing, and his master consented. He was gone three months. When he came back, he said that he had been to the Grand Banks, and went to setting type again as if only an afternoon had intervened.

I confess I was surprised to find that so many men spent their whole day, ay, their whole lives almost, a-fishing. It is remarkable what a serious business men make of getting their dinners, and how universally shiftlessness and a grovelling taste take refuge in a merely ant-like industry. Better go without your dinner, I thought, than be thus everlastingly fishing for it like a cormorant. Of course, *viewed from the shore*, our pursuits in the country appear not a whit less frivolous.

I once sailed three miles on a mackerel cruise myself. It was a Sunday evening after a very warm day in which there had been frequent thunder-showers, and I had walked along the shore from Cohasset to Duxbury. I wished to get over from the last place to Clark's Island, but no boat could stir, they said, at that stage of the tide, they being left high on the mud. At length I learned that the tavern-keeper, Winsor, was going out mackerelling with seven men that evening, and would take me. When there had been due delay, we one after another straggled down to the shore in a leisurely manner, as if waiting for the tide still, and in India-rubber boots, or carrying our shoes in our hands, waded to the boats, each of the crew bearing an armful of wood, and one a bucket of new potatoes besides. Then they resolved that each should bring one more armful of wood, and that would be enough. They had already got a barrel of water, and had some more in the schooner. We shoved the boats a dozen rods over the mud and water till they floated, then rowing half a mile to the vessel climbed aboard, and there we were in a mackerel schooner, a fine stout vessel of forty-three tons, whose name I forget. The baits were not dry on the hooks. There was the mill in which they ground the mackerel, and the trough to hold it, and the long-handled dipper to cast it overboard with; and already in the harbor we saw the surface rippled with schools of small mackerel, the real *Scomber vernalis*. The crew proceeded leisurely to weigh anchor and raise their two sails, there being a fair but very slight wind;—and the sun now setting clear and shining on the vessel after the thundershowers, I thought that I could not have commenced the voyage under more favorable auspices. They had four dories and commonly fished in them, else they fished on the starboard side aft where their fines hung ready, two to a man. The boom swung round once or twice, and Winsor cast overboard the foul juice of mackerel mixed with rain-water which remained in his trough, and then we gathered about the helmsman and told stories. I remember that the compass was affected by iron in its neighborhood and varied a few degrees. There was one among us just returned from California, who was now going as passenger for his health and amusement. They expected to be gone about a week, to begin fishing the next morning, and to carry their fish fresh to Boston. They landed me at Clark's Island, where the Pilgrims landed, for my companions wished to get some milk for the voyage. But I had seen the whole of it. The rest was only going to sea and catching the mackerel. Moreover, it was as well that I did not remain with them, considering the small quantity of supplies they had taken.

Now I saw the mackerel fleet *on its fishing-ground*, though I was not at first aware of it. So my experience was complete.

It was even more cold and windy to-day than before, and we were frequently glad to take shelter behind a sand-hill. None of the elements were resting. On the beach there is a ceaseless activity, always something going on, in storm and in calm, winter and summer, night and day. Even the sedentary man here enjoys a breadth of view which is almost equivalent to motion. In clear weather the laziest may look across the Bay as far as Plymouth at a glance, or over the Atlantic as far as human vision reaches, merely raising his eyelids; or if he is too lazy to look after all, he can hardly help hearing the ceaseless dash and roar of the breakers. The restless ocean may at any moment cast up a whale or a wrecked vessel at your feet. All the reporters in the world, the most rapid stenographers, could not report the news it brings. No creature could move slowly where there was so much life around. The few wreckers were either going or coming, and the ships and the sand-pipers, and the screaming gulls overhead; nothing stood still but the shore. The little beach-birds trotted past close to the water's edge, or paused but an instant to swallow their food, keeping time with the elements. I wondered how they ever got used to the sea, that they ventured so near the waves. Such tiny inhabitants the land brought forth! except one fox. And what could a fox do, looking on the Atlantic from that high bank? What is the sea to a fox? Sometimes we met a wrecker with his cart and dog,—and his dog's faint bark at us wayfarers, heard through the roaring of the surf, sounded ridiculously faint. To see a little trembling dainty-footed cur stand on the margin of the ocean, and ineffectually bark at a beach-bird, amid the roar of the Atlantic! Come with design to bark at a whale, perchance! That sound will do for farmyards. All the dogs looked out of place there, naked and as if shuddering at the vastness; and I thought that they would not have been there had it not been for the countenance of their masters. Still less could you think of a cat bending her steps that way, and shaking her wet foot over the Atlantic; yet even this happens sometimes, they tell me. In summer I saw the tender young of the Piping Plover, like chickens just hatched, mere pinches of down on two legs, running in troops, with a faint peep, along the edge of the waves. I used to see packs of half-wild dogs haunting the lonely beach on the south shore of Staten Island, in New York Bay, for the sake of the carrion there cast up; and I remember that once, when for a long time I had heard a furious barking in the tall grass of the marsh, a pack of half a dozen large dogs burst forth on to the beach, pursuing a little one which ran straight to me for protection, and I afforded it with some stones, though at some risk to myself; but the next day the little one was the first to bark at me. under these circumstances I could not but remember the words of the poet:—

> "Blow, blow, thou winter wind,
> Thou art not so unkind
>   As *his* ingratitude;
> Thy tooth is not so keen,
> Because thou art not seen,
>   Although thy breath be rude.
>
> "Freeze, freeze, thou bitter sky,
> Thou dost not bite so nigh
>   As benefits forgot;
> Though thou the waters warp,
> Thy sting is not so sharp
>   As friend remembered not."

Sometimes, when I was approaching the carcass of a horse or ox which lay on the beach there, where there was no living creature in sight, a dog would unexpectedly emerge from it and slink away with a mouthful of offal.

The sea-shore is a sort of neutral ground, a most advantageous point from which to contemplate this world. It is even a trivial place. The waves forever rolling to the land are too far-travelled and untamable to be familiar. Creeping along the endless beach amid the sun-squall and the foam, it occurs to us that we, too, are the product of sea-slime.

It is a wild, rank place, and there is no flattery in it. Strewn with crabs, horse-shoes, and razor-clams, and whatever the sea casts up,—a vast *morgue*, where famished dogs may range in packs, and crows come daily to glean the pittance which the tide leaves them. The carcasses of men and beasts together lie stately up upon its shelf, rotting and bleaching in the sun and waves, and each tide turns them in their beds, and tucks fresh sand under them. There is naked Nature, inhumanly sincere, wasting no thought on man, nibbling at the cliffy shore where gulls wheel amid the spray.

We saw this forenoon what, at a distance, looked like a bleached log with a branch still left on it. It proved to be one of the principal bones of a whale, whose carcass, having been stripped of blubber at sea and cut adrift, had been washed up some months before. It chanced that this was the most conclusive evidence which we met with to prove, what the Copenhagen antiquaries assert, that these shores were the *Furdustrandas* which Thorhall, the companion of Thorfinn during his expedition to Vinland in 1007. sailed past in disgust. It appears that after they had left the Cape and explored the country about Straum-Fiordr (Buzzards' Bay!), Thorhall, who was disappointed at not getting any wine to drink there, determined to sail north again in search of Vinland. Though the antiquaries have given us the original Icelandic. I prefer to quote their translation, since theirs is the only Latin which I know to have been aimed at Cape Cod.

> "Cum parati erant, sublato
> velo, cecinit Thorhallus:
> Eò redeamus, ubi conterranei
> sunt nostri! faciamus aliter,
> expansi arenosi peritum,
> lata navis explorare curricula:
> dum procellam incitantes gladii
> moræ impatientes, qui terram
> collaudant, Furdustrandas
> inhabitant et coquunt balænas."

In other words: "When they were ready and their sail hoisted, Thorhall sang: Let us return thither where our fellow-countrymen are. Let us make a bird[1] skilful to fly through the heaven of sand,[2] to explore the broad track of ships; while warriors who impel to the tempest of swords,[3] who praise the land, inhabit Wonder-Strands, *and cook whales.*'" And so he sailed north past Cape Cod, as the antiquaries say, "and was shipwrecked on to Ireland."

Though once there were more whales cast up here, I think that it was never more wild than now. We do not associate the idea of antiquity with the ocean, nor wonder how it looked a thousand years ago, as we do of the land, for it was equally wild and unfathomable always. The Indians have left no traces on its surface, but it is the same to the civilized man and the savage. The aspect of the shore only has changed. The ocean is a wilderness reaching round the globe, wilder than a Bengal jungle, and fuller of monsters, washing the very wharves of our cities and the gardens of our sea-side residences. Serpents, bears, hyenas, tigers, rapidly vanish as civilization advances, but the most populous and civilized city cannot scare a shark far from its wharves. It is no further advanced than Singapore, with its tigers, in this respect. The Boston papers had never told me that there were seals in the harbor. I had always associated these with the Esquimaux and other outlandish people. Yet from the parlor windows all along the coast you may see families of them sporting on the flats. They were as strange to me as the merman would be. Ladies who never walk in the woods, sail over the sea. To go to sea! Why, it is to have the experience of Noah,—to realize the deluge. Every vessel is an ark.

We saw no fences as we walked the beach, no birchen *riders*, highest of rails, projecting into the sea to keep the cows from wading round, nothing to remind us that man was proprietor of the shore. Yet a Truro man did tell us that owners of land on the east side of that town were regarded as owning the beach, in order that they might have the control of it so far as to defend themselves against the encroachments of the sand and the beach-grass,—for even this friend is sometimes regarded as a foe; but he said that this was not the case on the Bay side. Also I have seen in sheltered parts of the Bay temporary fences running to low-water mark, the posts being set in sills or sleepers placed transversely.

After we had been walking many hours, the mackerel fleet still hovered in the northern horizon nearly in the same direction, but farther off, hull down. Though their sails were set they never sailed away, nor yet came to anchor, but stood on various tacks as close together as vessels in a haven, and we in our ignorance thought that they were contending patiently with adverse winds, beating eastward; but we learned afterward that they were even then on their fishing-ground, and that they caught mackerel without taking in their mainsails or coming to anchor, "a smart breeze" (thence called a mackerel breeze) "being," as one says, "considered most favorable" for this purpose. We counted about two hundred sail of mackerel fishers within one small arc of the horizon, and a nearly equal number had disappeared southward. Thus they hovered about the extremity of the Cape, like moths round a candle; the lights at Race Point and Long Point being bright candles for them at night,—and at this distance they looked fair and white, as if they had not yet flown into the light, but nearer at hand afterward, we saw how some had formerly singed their wings and bodies.

A village seems thus, where its able-bodied men are all ploughing the ocean together, as a common field. In North Truro the women and girls may sit at their doors, and see where their husbands and brothers are harvesting their mackerel fifteen or twenty miles off, on the sea, with hundreds of white harvest wagons, just as in the country the farmers' wives sometimes see their husbands working in a distant hillside field. But the sound of no dinner-horn can reach the fisher's ear.

Having passed the narrowest part of the waist of the Cape, though still in Truro, for this township is about twelve miles long on the shore, we crossed over to the Bay side, not half a mile distant, in order to spend the noon on the nearest shrubby sand-hill in Provincetown, called Mount Ararat, which rises one hundred feet above the ocean. On our way thither we had occasion to admire the various beautiful forms and colors of the sand, and we noticed an interesting mirage, which I have since found that Hitchcock also observed on the sands of the Cape. We were crossing a shallow valley in the Desert, where the smooth and spotless sand sloped upward by a small angle to the horizon on every side, and at the lowest part was a long chain of clear but shallow pools. As we were approaching these for a drink in a diagonal direction across the valley, they appeared inclined at a slight but decided angle to the horizon, though they were plainly and broadly connected with one another, and there was not the least ripple to suggest a current; so that by the time we had reached a convenient part of one we seemed to have ascended several feet. They appeared to lie by magic on the side of the vale, like a mirror left in a slanting position. It was a very pretty mirage for a Provincetown desert, but not amounting to what, in Sanscrit, is called "the thirst of the gazelle," as there was real water here for a base, and we were able to quench our thirst after all.

Professor Rafn, of Copenhagen, thinks that the mirage which I noticed, but which an old inhabitant of Provincetown, to whom I mentioned it, had never seen nor heard of, had something to do with the name "Furdustrandas," i.e. Wonder-Strands, given, as I have said, in the old Icelandic account of Thorfinn's expedition to Vinland in the year 1007, to a part of the coast on which he landed. But these sands are more remarkable for their length than for their mirage, which is common to all deserts, and the reason for the name which the Northmen them-selves give,—"because it took a long time to sail by them,"—is sufficient and more applicable to these shores. However, if you should sail all the way from Greenland to Buzzards' Bay along the coast, you would get sight of a good many sandy beaches. But whether Thorfinn saw the mirage here or not, Thor-eau, one of the same family, did; and perchance it was because Lief the Lucky had, in a previous voyage, taken Thor-er and his people off the rock in the middle of the sea, that Thor-eau was born to see it.

This was not the only mirage which I saw on the Cape. That half of the beach next the bank is commonly level, or nearly so, while the other slopes downward to the water. As I was walking upon the edge of the bank in Wellfleet at sundown, it seemed to me that the inside half of the beach sloped upward toward the water to meet the other, forming a ridge ten or twelve feet high the whole length of the shore, but higher always opposite to where I stood; and I was not convinced of the contrary till I descended the bank, though the shaded outlines left by the waves of a previous tide but half-way down the apparent declivity might have taught me better. A stranger may easily detect what is strange to the oldest inhabitant, for the strange is his province. The old oysterman, speaking of gull-shooting, had said that you must aim under, when firing down the bank.

A neighbor tells me that one August, looking through a glass from Naushon to some vessels which were sailing along near Martha's Vineyard, the water about them appeared perfectly smooth, so that they were reflected in it, and yet their full sails proved that it must be rippled, and they who were with him thought that it was mirage, *i.e.* a reflection from a haze.

From the above-mentioned sand-hill we over-looked Provincetown and its harbor, now emptied of vessels, and also a wide expanse of ocean. As we did not wish to enter Provincetown before night, though it was cold and windy, we returned across the Deserts to the Atlantic side, and walked along the beach again nearly to Race Point, being still greedy of the sea influence. All the while it was not so calm as the reader may suppose, but it was blow, blow, blow,—roar, roar, roar,—tramp, tramp, tramp,—without interruption. The shore now trended nearly east and west.

Before sunset, having already seen the mackerel fleet returning into the Bay, we left the sea-shore on the north of Provincetown, and made our way across the Desert to the eastern extremity of the town. From the first high sand-hill, covered with beach-grass and bushes to its top, on the edge of the desert, we overlooked the shrubby hill and swamp country which surrounds Provincetown on the north, and protects it, in some measure, from the invading sand. Notwithstanding the universal barrenness, and the contiguity of the desert, I never saw an autumnal landscape so beautifully painted as this was. It was like the richest rug imaginable spread over an uneven surface; no damask nor velvet, nor Tyrian dye or stuffs, nor the work of any loom, could ever match it. There was the incredibly bright red of the Huckleberry, and the reddish brown of the Bayberry, mingled with the bright and living green of small Pitch-Pines, and also the duller green of the Bayberry, Boxberry, and Plum, the yellowish green of the Shrub-oaks, and the various golden and yellow and fawn-colored tints of the Birch and Maple and Aspen,—each making its own figure, and, in the midst, the few yellow sand-slides on the sides of the hills looked like the white floor seen through rents in the rug. Coming from the country as I did, and many autumnal woods as I had seen, this was perhaps the most novel and remarkable sight that I saw on the Cape. Probably the brightness of the tints was enhanced by contrast with the sand which surrounded this tract. This was a part of the furniture of Cape Cod. We had for days walked up the long and bleak piazza which runs along her Atlantic side, then over the sanded floor of her halls, and now we were being introduced into her boudoir. The hundred white sails crowding round Long Point into Provincetown Harbor, seen over the painted hills in front, looked like toy ships upon a mantel-piece.

The peculiarity of this autumnal landscape consisted in the lowness and thickness of the shrubbery, no less than in the brightness of the tints. It was like a thick stuff of worsted or a fleece, and looked as if a giant could take it up by the hem, or rather the tasselled fringe which trailed out on the sand, and shake it, though it needed not to be shaken. But no doubt the dust would fly in that case, for not a little has accumulated underneath it. Was it not such an autumnal landscape as this which suggested our high-colored rugs and carpets? Hereafter when I look on a richer rug than usual, and study its figures, I shall think, there are the huckleberry hills, and there the denser swamps of boxberry and blueberry: there the shrub-oak patches and the bayberries, there the maples and the birches and the pines. What other dyes are to be compared to these? They were warmer colors than I had associated with the New England coast.

After threading a swamp full of boxberry, and climbing several hills covered with shrub-oaks, without a path, where shipwrecked men would be in danger of perishing in the night, we came down upon the eastern extremity of the four planks which run the whole length of Provincetown street. This, which is the last town on the Cape, lies mainly in one street along the curving beach fronting the southeast. The sand-hills, covered with shrubbery and interposed with swamps and ponds, rose immediately behind it in the form of a crescent, which is from half a mile to a mile or more wide in the middle, and beyond these is the desert, which is the greater part of its territory, stretching to the sea on the east and west and north. The town is compactly built in the narrow space, from ten to fifty rods deep, between the harbor and the sand-hills, and contained at that time about twenty-six hundred inhabitants. The houses, in which a more modern and pretending style has at length prevailed over the fisherman's hut, stand on the inner or plank side of the street, and the fish and store houses, with the picturesque-looking windmills of the Salt-works, on the water side. The narrow portion of the beach between, forming the street, about eighteen feet wide, the only one where one carriage could pass another, if there was more than one carriage in the town, looked much "heavier" than any portion of the beach or the desert which we had walked on, it being above the reach of the highest tide, and the sand being kept loose by the occasional passage of a traveller. We learned that the four planks on which we were walking had been bought by the town's share of the Surplus Revenue, the disposition of which was a bone of contention between the inhabitants, till they wisely resolved thus to put it under foot. Yet some, it was said, were so provoked because they did not receive their particular share in money, that they persisted in walking in the sand a long time after the sidewalk was built. This is the only instance which I happen to know in which the surplus revenue proved a blessing to any town. A surplus revenue of dollars from the treasury to stem the greater evil of a surplus revenue of sand from the ocean. They expected to make a hard road by the time these planks were worn out. Indeed, they have already done so since we were there, and have almost forgotten their sandy baptism.

As we passed along we observed the inhabitants engaged in curing either fish or the coarse salt hay which they had brought home and spread on the beach before their doors, looking as yellow as if they had raked it out of the sea. The front-yard plots appeared like what indeed they were, portions of the beach fenced in, with Beach-grass growing in them, as if they were sometimes covered by the tide. You might still pick up shells and pebbles there. There were a few trees among the houses, especially silver abeles, willows, and balm-of-Gileads; and one man showed me a young oak which he had transplanted from behind the town, thinking it an apple-tree. But every man to his trade. Though he had little woodcraft, he was not the less weatherwise, and gave us one piece of information; viz., he had observed that when a thunder-cloud came up with a flood-tide it did not rain. This was the most completely maritime town that we were ever in. It was merely a good harbor, surrounded by land dry, if not firm,—an inhabited beach, whereon fishermen cured and stored their fish, without any back country. When ashore the inhabitants still walk on planks. A few small patches have been reclaimed from the swamps, containing commonly half a dozen square rods only each. We saw one which was fenced with four lengths of rail; also a fence made wholly of hogshead-staves stuck in the ground. These, and such as these, were all the cultivated and cultivable land in Provincetown. We were told that there were thirty or forty acres in all, but we did not discover a quarter part so much, and that was well dusted with sand, and looked as if the desert was claiming it. They are now turning some of their swamps into Cranberry Meadows on quite an extensive scale.

A cranberry meadow

Yet far from being out of the way. Provincetown is directly in the way of the navigator, and he is lucky who does not run afoul of it in the dark. It is situated on one of the highways of commerce, and men from all parts of the globe touch there in the course of a year.

The mackerel fleet had nearly all got in before us, it being Saturday night, excepting that division which had stood down towards Chatham in the morning; and from a hill where we went to see the sun set in the Bay we counted two hundred goodly looking schooners at anchor in the harbor at various distances from the shore, and more were yet coming round the Cape. As each came to anchor, it took in sail and swung round in the wind, and lowered its boat. They belonged chiefly to Wellfleet, Truro, and Cape Ann. This was that city of canvas which we had seen hull down in the horizon. Near at hand, and under bare poles, they were unexpectedly black-looking vessels, μέλαιναι νῆες. A fisherman told us that there were fifteen hundred vessels in the mackerel fleet, and that he had counted three hundred and fifty in Provincetown Harbor at one time. Being obliged to anchor at a considerable distance from the shore on account of the shallowness of the water, they made the impression of a larger fleet than the vessels at the wharves of a large city. As they had been manœuvring out there all day seemingly for our entertainment, while we were walking north-westward along the Atlantic, so now we found them flocking into Provincetown Harbor at night, just as we arrived, as if to meet us, and exhibit themselves close at hand. Standing by Race Point and Long Point with various speed, they reminded me of fowls coming home to roost.

These were genuine New England vessels. It is stated in the Journal of Moses Prince, a brother of the annalist, under date of 1721, at which time he visited Gloucester, that the first vessel of the class called schooner was built at Gloucester about eight years before, by Andrew Robinson; and late in the same century one Cotton Tufts gives us the tradition with some particulars, which he learned on a visit to the same place. According to the latter, Robinson having constructed a vessel which he masted and rigged in a peculiar manner, on her going off the stocks a bystander cried out, "*O, how she scoons!*" whereat Robinson replied, "*A schooner let her be!*" "From which time," says Tufts, "vessels thus masted and rigged have gone by the name of schooners; before which, vessels of this description were not known in Europe." (See Mass. Hist. Coll., Vol. IX., 1st Series, and Vol. I., 4th Series.) Yet I can hardly believe this, for a schooner has always seemed to me—the typical vessel.

According to C. E. Potter of Manchester, New Hampshire, the very word *schooner* is of New England origin, being from the Indian *schoon* or *scoot*, meaning to rush, as Schoodic, from *scoot* and *anke*, a place where water rushes. N. B. Somebody of Gloucester was to read a paper on this matter before a genealogical society, in Boston, March 3, 1859, according to the *Boston Journal*, q. v.

Nearly all who come out must walk on the four planks which I have mentioned, so that you are pretty sure to meet all the inhabitants of Provincetown who come out in the course of a day, provided you keep out yourself. This evening the planks were crowded with mackerel fishers, to whom we gave and from whom we took the wall, as we returned to our hotel. This hotel was kept by a tailor, his shop on the one side of the door, his hotel on the other, and his day seemed to be divided between carving meat and carving broadcloth.

The next morning, though it was still more cold and blustering than the day before, we took to the Deserts again, for we spent our days wholly out of doors, in the sun when there was any, and in the wind which never failed. After threading the shrubby hill country at the southwest end of the town, west of the Shank-Painter Swamp, whose expressive name—for we understood it at first as a landsman naturally would—gave it importance in our eyes, we crossed the sands to the shore south of Race Point and three miles distant, and thence roamed round eastward through the desert to where we had left the sea the evening before. We travelled five or six miles after we got out there, on a curving line, and might have gone nine or ten, over vast platters of pure sand, from the midst of which we could not see a particle of vegetation, excepting the distant thin fields of Beach-grass, which crowned and made the ridges toward which the sand sloped upward on each side;—all the while in the face of a cutting wind as cold as January; indeed, we experienced no weather so cold as this for nearly two months afterward. This desert extends from the extremity of the Cape, through Provincetown into Truro, and many a time as we were traversing it we were reminded of "Riley's Narrative" of his captivity in the sands of Arabia, notwithstanding the cold. Our eyes magnified the patches of Beach-grass into cornfields in the horizon, and we probably exaggerated the height of the ridges on account of the mirage. I was pleased to learn afterward, from Kalm's Travels in North America, that the inhabitants of the Lower St. Lawrence call this grass (*Calamagrostis arenaria*), and also Sea-lyme grass (*Elymus arenarius*), *seigle de me*; and he adds, "I have been assured that these plants grow in great plenty in Newfoundland, and on other North American shores; the places covered with them looking, at a distance, like cornfields; which might explain the passage in our northern accounts [he wrote in 1749] of the excellent wine land [*Vinland det goda*, Translator], which mentions that they had found whole fields of wheat growing wild."

The Beach-grass is "two to four feet high, of a seagreen color," and it is said to be widely diffused over the world. In the Hebrides it is used for mats, pack-saddles, bags, hats, etc.; paper has been made of it at Dorchester in this State, and cattle eat it when tender. It has heads somewhat like rye, from six inches to a foot in length, and it is propagated both by roots and seeds. To express its love for sand, some botanists have called it *Psamma arenaria*, which is the Greek for sand, qualified by the Latin for sandy,—or sandy sand. As it is blown about by the wind, while it is held fast by its roots, it describes myriad circles in the sand as accurately as if they were made by compasses.

It was the dreariest scenery imaginable. The only animals which we saw on the sand at that time were spiders, which are to be found almost everywhere whether on snow or ice-water or sand,—and a venomous-looking, long, narrow worm, one of the myriapods, or thousand-legs. We were surprised to see spider-holes in that flowing sand with an edge as firm as that of a stoned well.

In June this sand was scored with the tracks of turtles both large and small, which had been out in the night, leading to and from the swamps. I was told by a *terræ filius* who has a "farm" on the edge of the desert, and is familiar with the fame of Provincetown, that one man had caught twenty-five snapping-turtles there the previous spring. His own method of catching them was to put a toad on a mackerel-hook and cast it into a pond, tying the line to a stump or stake on shore.

Invariably the turtle when hooked crawled up the line to the stump, and was found waiting there by his captor, however long afterward. He also said that minks, muskrats, foxes, coons, and wild mice were found there, but no squirrels. We heard of sea-turtle as large as a barrel being found on the beach and on East Harbor marsh, but whether they were native there, or had been lost out of some vessel, did not appear. Perhaps they were the Salt-water Terrapin, or else the Smooth Terrapin, found thus far north. Many toads were met with where there was nothing but sand and beach-grass. In Truro I had been surprised at the number of large light-colored toads everywhere hopping over the dry and sandy fields, their color corresponding to that of the sand. Snakes also are common on these pure sand beaches, and I have never been so much troubled by mosquitoes as in such localities. At the same season strawberries grew there abundantly in the little hollows on the edge of the desert standing amid the beach-grass in the sand, and the fruit of the shadbush or Amelanchier, which the inhabitants call Josh-pears (some think from juicy?), is very abundant on the hills. I fell in with an obliging man who conducted me to the best locality for strawberries. He said that he would not have shown me the place if he had not seen that I was a stranger, and could not anticipate him another year; I therefore feel bound in honor not to reveal it. When we came to a pond, he being the native did the honors and carried me over on his shoulders, like Sindbad. One good turn deserves another, and if he ever comes our way I will do as much for him.

In one place we saw numerous dead tops of trees projecting through the otherwise uninterrupted desert, where, as we afterward learned, thirty or forty years before a flourishing forest had stood, and now, as the trees were laid bare from year to year, the inhabitants cut off their tops for fuel.

We saw nobody that day outside of the town; it was too wintry for such as had seen the Backside before, or for the greater number who never desire to see it, to venture out; and we saw hardly a track to show that any had ever crossed this desert. Yet I was told that some are always out on the Back-side night and day in severe weather, looking for wrecks, in order that they may get the job of discharging the cargo, or the like,—and thus shipwrecked men are succored. But, generally speaking, the inhabitants rarely visit these sands. One who had lived in Provincetown thirty years told me that he had not been through to the north side within that time. Sometimes the natives themselves come near perishing by losing their way in snow-storms behind the town.

The wind was not a Sirocco or Simoon, such as we associate with the desert, but a New England northeaster,—and we sought shelter in vain under the sand-hills, for it blew all about them, rounding them into cones, and was sure to find us out on whichever side we sat. From time to time we lay down and drank at little pools in the sand, filled with pure fresh water, all that was left, probably, of a pond or swamp. The air was filled with dust like snow, and cutting sand which made the face tingle, and we saw what it must be to face it when the weather was drier, and, if possible, windier still,—to face a migrating sand-bar in the air, which has picked up its duds and is off,—to be whipped with a cat, not o' nine-tails, but of a myriad of tails, and each one a sting to it. A Mr. Whitman, a former minister of Wellfleet, used to write to his inland friends that the blowing sand scratched the windows so that he was obliged to have one new pane set every week, that he might see out.

On the edge of the shrubby woods the sand had the appearance of an inundation which was overwhelming them, terminating in an abrupt bank many feet higher than the surface on which they stood, and having partially buried the out-side trees. The moving sand-hills of England, called Dunes or Downs, to which these have been likened, are either formed of sand cast up by the sea, or of sand taken from the land itself in the first place by the wind, and driven still farther inward. It is here a tide of sand impelled by waves and wind, slowly flowing from the sea toward the town. The northeast winds are said to be the strongest, but the northwest to move most sand, because they are the driest. On the shore of the Bay of Biscay many villages were formerly destroyed in this way. Some of the ridges of beach-grass which we saw were planted by government many years ago, to preserve the harbor of Provincetown and the extremity of the Cape. I talked with some who had been employed in the planting. In the "Description of the Eastern

Coast," which I have already referred to, it is said: "Beach-grass during the spring and summer grows about two feet and a half. If surrounded by naked beach, the storms of autumn and winter heap up the sand on all sides, and cause it to rise nearly to the top of the plant. In the ensuing spring the grass mounts anew; is again covered with sand in the winter; and thus a hill or ridge continues to ascend as long as there is a sufficient base to support it, or till the circumscribing sand, being also covered with beach-grass, will no longer yield to the force of the winds." Sand-hills formed in this way are sometimes one hundred feet high and of every variety of form, like snow-drifts, or Arab tents, and are continually shifting. The grass roots itself very firmly. When I endeavored to pull it up, it usually broke off ten inches or a foot below the surface, at what had been the surface the year before, as appeared by the numerous offshoots there, it being a straight, hard, round shoot, showing by its length how much the sand had accumulated the last year; and sometimes the dead stubs of a previous season were pulled up with it from still deeper in the sand, with their own more decayed shoot attached,—so that the age of a sand-hill, and its rate of increase for several years, is pretty accurately recorded in this way.

The sand dunes drifting in upon the trees

Old Gerard, the English herbalist, says, p. 1250: "I find mention in Stowe's Chronicle, in Anno 1555, of a certain pulse or pease, as they term it, wherewith the poor people at that time, there being a great dearth, were miraculously helped: he thus mentions it. In the month of August (saith he), in Suffolke, at a place by the sea side all of hard stone and pibble, called in those parts a shelf, lying between the towns of Orford and Aldborough, where neither grew grass nor any earth was ever seen; it chanced in this barren place suddenly to spring up without any tillage or sowing, great abundance of peason, whereof the poor gathered (as men judged) above one hundred quarters, yet remained some ripe and some blossoming, as many as ever there were before: to the which place rode the Bishop of Norwich and the Lord Willoughby, with others in great number, who found nothing but hard, rocky stone the space of three yards under the roots of these peason, which roots were great and long, and very sweet." He tells us also that Gesner learned from Dr. Cajus that there were enough there to supply thousands of men. He goes on to say that "they without doubt grew there many years before, but were not observed till hunger made them take notice of them, and quickened their invention, which commonly in our people is very dull, especially in finding out food of this nature. My worshipful friend Dr. Argent hath told me that many years ago he was in this place, and caused his man to pull among the beach with his hands, and follow the roots so long until he got some equal in length unto his height, yet could come to no ends of them." Gerard never saw them, and is not certain what kind they were.

In Dwight's Travels in New England it is stated that the inhabitants of Truro were formerly regularly warned under the authority of law in the month of April yearly, to plant beachgrass, as elsewhere they are warned to repair the highways. They dug up the grass in bunches, which were afterward divided into several smaller ones, and set about three feet apart, in rows, so arranged as to break joints and obstruct the passage of the wind. It spread itself rapidly, the weight of the seeds when ripe bending the heads of the grass, and so dropping directly by its side and vegetating there. In this way, for instance, they built up again that part of the Cape between Truro and Provincetown where the sea broke over in the last century. They have now a public road near there, made by laying sods, which were full of roots, bottom upward and close together on the sand, double in the middle of the track, then spreading brush evenly over the sand on each side for half a dozen feet, planting beachgrass on the banks in regular rows, as above described, and sticking a fence of brush against the hollows.

The attention of the general government was first attracted to the danger which threatened Cape Cod Harbor from the inroads of the sand, about thirty years ago, and commissioners were at that time appointed by Massachusetts, to examine the premises. They reported in June, 1825, that, owing to "the trees and brush having been cut down, and the beach-grass destroyed on the seaward side of the Cape, opposite the Harbor," the original surface of the ground had been broken up and removed by the wind toward the Harbor,—during the previous fourteen years,—over an extent of "one half a mile in breadth, and about four and a half miles in length."—"The space where a few years since were some of the highest lands on the Cape, covered with trees and bushes," presenting "an extensive waste of undulating sand ";—and that, during the previous twelve months, the sand "had approached the Harbor an average distance of fifty rods, for an extent of four and a half miles!" and unless some measures were adopted to check its progress, it would in a few years destroy both the harbor and the town. They therefore recommended that beach-grass be set out on a curving line over a space ten rods wide and four and a half miles long, and that cattle, horses, and sheep be prohibited from going abroad, and the inhabitants from cutting the brush.

I was told that about thirty thousand dollars in all had been appropriated to this object, though it was complained that a great part of this was spent foolishly, as the public money is wont to be. Some say that while the government is planting beach-grass behind the town for the protection of the harbor, the inhabitants are rolling the sand into the harbor in wheelbarrows, in order to make house-lots. The Patent-Office has recently imported the seed of this grass from Holland, and distributed it over the country, but probably we have as much as the Hollanders.

Thus Cape Cod is anchored to the heavens, as it were, by a myriad little cables of beach-grass, and, if they should fail, would become a total wreck, and erelong go to the bottom. Formerly, the cows were permitted to go at large, and they ate many strands of the cable by which the Cape is moored, and well-nigh set it adrift, as the bull did the boat which was moored with a grass rope; but now they are not permitted to wander.

A portion of Truro which has considerable taxable property on it has lately been added to Provincetown, and I was told by a Truro man that his townsmen talked of petitioning the legislature to set off the next mile of their territory also to Provincetown, in order that she might have her share of the lean as well as the fat, and take care of the road through it; for its whole value is literally to hold the Cape together, and even this it has not always done. But Provincetown strenuously declines the gift.

The wind blowed so hard from the northeast that, cold as it was, we resolved to see the breakers on the Atlantic side, whose din we had heard all the morning; so we kept on eastward through the Desert, till we struck the shore again northeast of Provincetown, and exposed ourselves to the full force of the piercing blast. There are extensive shoals there over which the sea broke with great force. For half a mile from the shore it was one mass of white breakers, which, with the wind, made such a din that we could hardly hear ourselves speak. Of this part of the coast it is said: "A northeast storm, the most violent and fatal to seamen, as it is frequently accompanied with snow, blows directly on the land: a strong current sets along the shore; add to which that ships, during the operation of such a storm, endeavor to work northward, that they may get into the bay. Should they be unable to weather Race Point, the wind drives them on the shore, and a shipwreck is inevitable. Accordingly, the strand is everywhere covered with the fragments of vessels." But since the Highland Light was erected, this part of the coast is less dangerous, and it is said that more shipwrecks occur south of that light, where they were scarcely known before.

The white breakers on the Atlantic side

This was the stormiest sea that we witnessed,—more *tumultuous*, my companion affirmed, than the rapids of Niagara, and, of course, on a far greater scale. It was the ocean in a gale, a clear, cold day, with only one sail in sight, which labored much, as if it were anxiously seeking a harbor. It was high tide when we reached the shore, and in one place, for a considerable distance, each wave dashed up so high that it was difficult to pass between it and the bank. Further south, where the bank was higher, it would have been dangerous to attempt it. A native of the Cape has told me that, many years ago, three boys, his playmates, having gone to this beach in Wellfleet to visit a wreck, when the sea receded ran down to the wreck, and when it came in ran before it to the bank, but the sea following fast at their heels, caused the bank to cave and bury them alive.

It was the roaring sea, θάλασσα ἠχήεσσα,—

ἀμφὶ δὲ τ' ἄκραι
Ἠϊόνες βοόωσιν, ἐρευγομένης ἁλὸς ἔξω.

And the summits of the bank
Around resound, the sea being vomited forth.

As we stood looking on this scene we were gradually convinced that fishing here and in a pond were not, in all respects, the same, and that he who waits for fair weather and a calm sea may never see the glancing skin of a mackerel, and get no nearer to a cod than the wooden emblem in the State House.

Having lingered on the shore till we were well-nigh chilled to death by the wind, and were ready to take shelter in a Charity-house, we turned our weather-beaten faces toward Provincetown and the Bay again, having now more than doubled the Cape.

[1] *I. e.* a vessel.

[2] The sea, which is arched over its sandy bottom like a heaven.

[3] Battle.

## X

## PROVINCETOWN

Early the next morning I walked into a fish-house near our hotel, where three or four men were engaged in trundling out the pickled fish on barrows, and spreading them to dry. They told me that a vessel had lately come in from the Banks with forty-four thousand codfish. Timothy Dwight says that, just before he arrived at Provincetown, "a schooner come in from the Great Bank with fifty-six thousand fish, almost one thousand five hundred quintals, taken in a single voyage; the main deck being, on her return, eight inches under water in calm weather." The cod in this fish-house, just out of the pickle, lay packed several feet deep, and three or four men stood on them in cowhide boots, pitching them on to the barrows with an instrument which had a single iron point. One young man, who chewed tobacco, spat on the fish repeatedly. Well, sir, thought I, when that older man sees you he will speak to you. But presently I saw the older man do the same thing. It reminded me of the figs of Smyrna. "How long does it take to cure these fish? I asked.

"Two good drying days, sir," was the answer.

I walked across the street again into the hotel to breakfast, and mine host inquired if I would take "hashed fish or beans." I took beans, though they never were a favorite dish of mine. I found next summer that this was still the only alternative proposed here, and the landlord was still ringing the changes on these two words. In the former dish there was a remarkable proportion of fish. As you travel inland the potato predominates. It chanced that I did not taste fresh fish of any kind on the Cape, and I was assured that they were not so much used there as in the country. That is where they are cured, and where, sometimes, travellers are cured of eating them. No fresh meat was slaughtered in Provincetown, but the little that was used at the public houses was brought from Boston by the steamer.

In Provincetown harbor

A great many of the houses here were surrounded by fish-flakes close up to the sills on all sides, with only a narrow passage two or three feet wide, to the front door; so that instead of looking out into a flower or grass plot, you looked on to so many square rods of cod turned wrong side outwards. These parterres were said to be least like a flower-garden in a good drying day in mid-summer. There were flakes of every age and pattern, and some so rusty and overgrown with lichens that they looked as if they might have served the founders of the fishery here. Some had broken down under the weight of successive harvests. The principal employment of the inhabitants at this time seemed to be to trundle out their fish and spread them in the morning, and bring them in at night. I saw how many a loafer who chanced to be out early enough got a job at wheeling out the fish of his neighbor who was anxious to improve the whole of a fair day. Now, then, I knew where salt fish were caught. They were everywhere lying on their backs, their collar-bones standing out like the lapels of a man-o'-war-man's jacket, and inviting all things to come and rest in their bosoms; and all things, with a few exceptions, accepted the invitation. I think, by the way, that if you should wrap a large salt fish round a small boy, he would have a coat of such a fashion as I have seen many a one wear to muster. Salt fish were stacked up on the wharves, looking like corded wood, maple and yellow birch with the bark left on. I mistook them for this at first, and such in one sense they were,—fuel to maintain our vital fires,—an eastern wood which grew on the Grand Banks. Some were stacked in the form of huge flower-pots, being laid in small circles with the tails outwards, each circle successively larger than the preceding until the pile was three or four feet high, when the circles rapidly diminished, so as to form a conical roof. On the shores of New Brunswick this is covered with birch-bark, and stones are placed upon it, and being thus rendered impervious to the rain, it is left to season before being packed for exportation.

It is rumored that in the fall the cows here are sometimes fed on cod's-heads! The godlike part of the cod, which, like the human head, is curiously and wonderfully made, forsooth has but little less brain in it,—coming; to such an end I to be craunched by cows I I felt my own skull crack from sympathy. What if the heads of men were to be cut off to feed the cows of a superior order of beings who inhabit the islands in the ether? Away goes your fine brain, the house of thought and instinct, to swell the cud of a ruminant animal!—However, an inhabitant assured me that they did not make a practice of feeding cows on cod's-heads; the cows merely would eat them sometimes; but I might live there all my days and never see it done. A cow wanting salt would also sometimes lick out all the soft part of a cod on the flakes. This he would have me believe was the foundation of this fish-story.

It has been a constant traveller's tale and perhaps slander, now for thousands of years, the Latins and Greeks have repeated it, that this or that nation feeds its cattle, or horses, or sheep, on fish, as may be seen in OElian and Pliny, but in the Journal of Nearchus, who was Alexander's admiral, and made a voyage from the Indus to the Euphrates three hundred and twenty-six years before Christ, it is said that the inhabitants of a portion of the intermediate coast, whom he called Ichthyophagi or Fish-eaters, not only ate fishes raw and also dried and pounded in a whale's vertebra for a mortar and made into a paste, but gave them to their cattle, there being no grass on the coast;

and several modern travellers—Braybosa, Niebuhr, and others—make the same report. Therefore in balancing the evidence I am still in doubt about the Provincetown cows. As for other domestic animals. Captain King in his continuation of Captain Cook's Journal in 1779, says of the dogs of Kamtschatka, "Their food in the winter consists entirely of the heads, entrail, and backbones of salmon, which are put aside and dried for that purpose; and with this diet they are fed but sparingly." (Cook's Journal, Vol. VII., p. 315.)

As we are treating of fishy matters, let me insert what Pliny says, that "the commanders of the fleets of Alexander the Great have related that the Gedrosi, who dwell on the banks of the river Arabis, are in the habit of making the doors of their houses with the jaw-bones of fishes, and raftering the roofs with their bones." Strabo tells the same of the Ichthyophagi. "Hardouin remarks that the Basques of his day were in the habit of fencing their gardens with the ribs of the whale, which sometimes exceeded twenty feet in length; and Cuvier says that at the present time the jaw-bone of the whale is used in Norway for the purpose of making beams or posts for buildings." (Bohn's ed., trans, of Pliny, Vol. II., p. 361.) Herodotus says the inhabitants on Lake Prasias in Thrace (living on piles) "give fish for fodder to their horses and beasts of burden."

Provincetown was apparently what is called a flourishing town. Some of the inhabitants asked me if I did not think that they appeared to be well off generally. I said that I did, and asked how many there were in the almshouse. "O, only one or two, infirm or idiotic," answered they. The outward aspect of the houses and shops frequently suggested a poverty which their interior comfort and even richness disproved. You might meet a lady daintily dressed in the Sabbath morning, wading in among the sandhills, from church, where there appeared no house fit to receive her, yet no doubt the interior of the house answered to the exterior of the lady. As for the interior of the inhabitants I am still in the dark about it. I had a little intercourse with some whom I met in the street, and was often agreeably disappointed by discovering the intelligence of rough, and what would be considered unpromising specimens. Nay, I ventured to call on one citizen the next summer, by special invitation. I found him sitting in his front doorway, that Sabbath evening, prepared for me to come in unto him; but unfortunately for his reputation for keeping open house, there was stretched across his gateway a circular cobweb of the largest kind and quite entire. This looked so ominous that I actually turned aside and went in the back way.

This Monday morning was beautifully mild and calm, both on land and water, promising us a smooth passage across the Bay, and the fishermen feared that it would not be so good a drying day as the cold and windy one which preceded it. There could hardly have been a greater contrast. This was the first of the Indian summer days, though at a late hour in the morning we found the wells in the sand behind the town still covered with ice, which had formed in the night. What with wind and sun my most prominent feature fairly cast its slough. But I assure you it will take more than two good drying days to cure me of rambling. After making an excursion among the hills in the neighborhood of the Shank-Painter Swamp, and getting a little work done in its line, we took our seat upon the highest sand-hill overlooking the town, in mid-air, on a long plank stretched across between two hillocks of sand, where some boys were endeavoring in vain to fly their kite; and there we remained the rest of that forenoon looking out over the placid harbor, and watching for the first appearance of the steamer from Wellfleet, that we might be in readiness to go on board when we heard the whistle off Long Point.

We got what we could out of the boys in the meanwhile. Provincetown boys are of course all sailors and have sailors' eyes. When we were at the Highland Light the last summer, seven or eight miles from Provincetown Harbor, and wished to know one Sunday morning if the *Olata*, a well-known yacht, had got in from Boston, so that we could return in her, a Provincetown boy about ten years old, who chanced to be at the table, remarked that she had. I asked him how he knew. "I just saw her come in," said he. When I expressed surprise that he could distinguish her from other vessels so far, he said that there were not so many of those two-topsail schooners about but that he could tell her. Palfrey said, in his oration at Barnstable, the duck does not take to the water with a surer instinct than the Barnstable boy. [He might have said the Cape Cod boy as well.] He leaps from his leading-strings into the shrouds, it is but a bound from the mother's lap to the masthead. He boxes the compass in his infant soliloquies. He can hand, reef, and steer by the time he flies a kite.

This was the very day one would have chosen to sit upon a hill overlooking sea and land, and muse there. The mackerel fleet was rapidly taking its departure, one schooner after another, and standing round the Cape, like fowls leaving their roosts in the morning to disperse themselves in distant fields. The turtle-like sheds of the salt-works were crowded into every nook in the hills, immediately behind the town, and their now idle windmills lined the shore. It was worth the while to see by what coarse and simple chemistry this almost necessary of life is obtained, with the sun for journeyman, and a single apprentice to do the chores for a large establishment. It is a sort of tropical labor, pursued too in the sunniest season; more interesting than gold or diamond-washing, which, I fancy, it somewhat resembles at a distance. In the production of the necessaries of life Nature is ready enough to assist man. So at the potash works which I have seen at Hull, where they burn the stems of the kelp and boil the ashes. Verily, chemistry is not a splitting of hairs when you have got half a dozen raw Irishmen in the laboratory. It is said, that owing to the reflection of the sun from the sand-hills, and there being absolutely no fresh water emptying into the harbor, the same number of superficial feet yields more salt here than in any other part of the county. A little rain is considered necessary to clear the air, and make salt fast and good, for as paint does not dry, so water does not evaporate in dog-day weather. But they were now, as elsewhere on the Cape, breaking up their salt-works and selling them for lumber.

From that elevation we could overlook the operations of the inhabitants almost as completely as if the roofs had been taken off. They were busily covering the wicker-worked flakes about their houses with salted fish, and we now saw that the back yards were improved for this purpose as much as the front; where one man's fish ended another's began. In almost every yard we detected some little building from which these treasures were being trundled forth and systematically spread, and we saw that there was an art as well as a knack even in spreading fish, and that a division of labor was profitably practised. One man was withdrawing his fishes a few inches beyond the nose of his neighbor's cow which had stretched her neck over a paling to get at them. It seemed a quite domestic employment, like drying clothes, and indeed in some parts of the county the women take part in it.

I noticed in several places on the Cape a sort of clothes-*flakes*. They spread brush on the ground, and fence it round, and then lay their clothes on it, to keep them from the sand. This is a Cape Cod clothes-yard.

The sand is the great enemy here. The tops of some of the hills were enclosed and a board put up, forbidding all persons entering the enclosure, lest their feet should disturb the sand, and set it a-blowing or a-sliding. The inhabitants are obliged to get leave from the authorities to cut wood behind the town for fish-flakes, bean-poles, pea-brush, and the like, though, as we were told, they may transplant trees from one part of the township to another without leave. The sand drifts like snow, and sometimes the lower story of a house is concealed by it, though it is kept off by a wall. The houses were formerly built on piles, in order that the driving sand might pass under them. We saw a few old ones here still standing on their piles, but they were boarded up now, being protected by their younger neighbors. There was a school-house, just under the hill on which we sat, filled with sand up to the tops of the desks, and of course the master and scholars had fled. Perhaps they had imprudently left the windows open one day, or neglected to mend a broken pane. Yet in one place was advertised "Fine sand for sale here,"—I could hardly believe my eyes,—probably some of the street sifted,—a good instance of the fact that a man confers a value on the most worthless thing by mixing himself with it, according to which rule we must have conferred a value on the whole back-side of Cape Cod;—but I thought that if they could have advertised "Fat Soil," or perhaps "Fine sand got rid of," ay, and "Shoes emptied here," it would have been more alluring. As we looked down on the town, I thought that I saw one man, who probably lived beyond the extremity of the planking, steering and tacking for it in a sort of snow-shoes, but I may have been mistaken. In some pictures of Provincetown the persons of the inhabitants are not drawn below the ankles, so much being supposed to be buried in the sand. Nevertheless, natives of Provincetown assured me that they could walk in the middle of the road without trouble even in slippers, for they had learned how to put their feet down and lift them up without taking in any sand. One man said that he should be surprised if he found half a dozen grains of sand in his pumps at night, and stated, moreover, that the young ladies had a dexterous way of emptying their shoes at each step, which it would take a stranger a long time to learn. The tires of the stage-wheels were about five inches wide; and the wagon-tires generally on the Cape are an inch or two wider, as the sand is an inch or two deeper than elsewhere. I saw a baby's wagon with tires six inches wide to keep it near the surface. The more tired the wheels, the less tired the horses. Yet all the time that we were in Provincetown, which was two days and nights, we saw only one horse and cart, and they were conveying a coffin. They did not try such experiments there on common occasions. The next summer I saw only the two-wheeled horse-cart which conveyed me thirty rods into the harbor on my way to the steamer. Yet we read that there were two horses and two yoke of oxen here in 1791, and we were told that there were several more when we were there, beside the stage team. In Barber's Historical Collections, it is said, "So rarely are wheel-carriages seen in the place that they are a matter of some curiosity to the younger part of the community. A lad who understood navigating the ocean much better than land travel, on seeing a man driving a wagon in the street, expressed his surprise at his being able to drive so straight without the assistance of a rudder." There was no rattle of carts, and there would have been no rattle if there had been any carts. Some saddle-horses that passed the hotel in the evening merely made the sand fly with a rustling sound like a writer sanding his paper copiously, but there was no sound of their tread. No doubt there are more horses and carts there at present, A sleigh is never seen, or at least is a great novelty on the Cape, the snow being either absorbed by the sand or blown into drifts.

Nevertheless, the inhabitants of the Cape generally do not complain of their "soil," but will tell you that it is good enough for them to dry their fish on.

Notwithstanding all this sand, we counted three meeting-houses, and four school-houses nearly as large, on this street, though some had a tight board fence about them to preserve the plot within level and hard. Similar fences, even within a foot of many of the houses, gave the town a less cheerful and hospitable appearance than it would otherwise have had. They told us that, on the whole, the sand had made no progress for the last ten years, the cows being no longer permitted to go at large, and every means being taken to stop the sandy tide.

In 1727 Provincetown was "invested with peculiar privileges." for its encouragement. Once or twice it was nearly abandoned; but now lots on the street fetch a high price, though titles to them were first obtained by possession and improvement, and they are still transferred by quitclaim deeds merely, the township being the property of the State. But though lots were so valuable on the street, you might in many places throw a stone over them to where a man could still obtain land, or sand, by squatting on or improving it.

Provincetown—A bit of the village from the wharf

Stones are very rare on the Cape. I saw a very few small stones used for pavements and for bank walls, in one or two places in my walk, but they are so scarce that, as I was informed, vessels have been forbidden to take them from the beach for ballast, and therefore their crews used to land at night and steal them. I did not hear of a rod of regular stone wall below Orleans. Yet I saw one man underpinning a new house in Eastham with some "rocks," as he called them, which he said a neighbor had collected with great pains in the course of years, and finally made over to him. This I thought was a gift worthy of being recorded,—equal to a transfer of California "rocks," almost. Another man who was assisting him, and who seemed to be a close observer of nature, hinted to me the locality of a rock in that neighborhood which was "forty-two paces in circumference and fifteen feet high," for he saw that I was a stranger, and, probably, would not carry it off. Yet I suspect that the locality of the few large rocks on the forearm of the Cape is well known to the inhabitants generally. I even met with one man who had got a smattering of mineralogy, but where he picked it up I could not guess. I thought that he would meet with some interesting geological nuts for him to crack, if he should ever visit the mainland, Cohasset, or Marblehead for instance.

The well stones at the Highland Light were brought from Hingham, but the wells and cellars of the Cape are generally built of brick, which also are imported. The cellars, as well as the wells, are made in a circular form, to prevent the sand from pressing in the wall. The former are only from nine to twelve feet in diameter, and are said to be very cheap, since a single tier of brick will suffice for a cellar of even larger dimensions. Of course, if you live in the sand, you will not require a large cellar to hold your roots. In Provincetown, when formerly they suffered the sand to drive under their houses, obliterating all rudiments of a cellar, they did not raise a vegetable to put into one. One farmer in Wellfleet, who raised fifty bushels of potatoes, showed me his cellar under a corner of his house, not more than nine feet in diameter, looking like a cistern: but he had another of the same size under his barn.

You need dig only a few feet almost anywhere near the shore of the Cape to find fresh water. But that which we tasted was invariably poor. though the inhabitants called it good, as if they were comparing it with salt water. In the account of Truro, it is said. "Wells dug near the shore are dry at low water, or rather at what is called young flood, but are replenished with the flowing of the tide,"— the salt water, which is lowest in the sand, apparently forcing the fresh up. When you express your surprise at the greenness of a Provincetown garden on the beach, in a dry season, they will sometimes tell you that the tide forces the moisture up to them. It is an interesting fact that low sand-bars in the midst of the ocean, perhaps even those which are laid bare only at low tide, are reservoirs of fresh water at which the thirsty mariner can supply himself. They appear, like huge sponges, to hold the rain and dew which fall on them, and which, by capillary attraction, are prevented from mingling with the surrounding brine.

The Harbor of Provincetown—which, as well as the greater part of the Bay, and a wide expanse of ocean, we overlooked from our perch—is deservedly famous. It opens to the south, is free from rocks, and is never frozen over. It is said that the only ice seen in it drifts in sometimes from Barnstable or Plymouth. Dwight remarks that "The storms which prevail on the American coast generally come from the east; and there is no other harbor on a windward shore within two hundred miles." J. D. Graham, who has made a very minute and thorough survey of this harbor and the adjacent waters, states that "its capacity, depth of water, excellent anchorage, and the complete shelter it affords from all winds, combine to render it one of the most valuable ship harbors on our coast." It is *the* harbor of the Cape and of the fishermen of Massachusetts generally. It was known to navigators several years at least before the settlement of Plymouth. In Captain John Smith's map of New England, dated 1614. it bears the name of Milford Haven, and Massachusetts Bay that of Stuard's Bay. His Highness, Prince Charles, changed the name of Cape Cod to Cape James; but even princes have not always power to change a name for the worse, and as Cotton Mather said, Cape Cod is "a name which I suppose it will never lose till shoals of codfish be seen swimming on its highest hills."

Many an early voyager was unexpectedly caught by this hook, and found himself embayed. On successive maps, Cape Cod appears sprinkled over with French, Dutch, and English names, as it made part of New France, New Holland, and New England. On one map Provincetown Harbor is called "Fuic (bownet?) Bay," Barnstable Bay "Staten Bay," and the sea north of it "Mare del Noort," or the North Sea. On another, the extremity of the Cape is called "Staten Hoeck," or the States Hook. On another, by Young, this has Noord Zee, Staten hoeck or Hit hoeck, but the copy at Cambridge has no date; the whole Cape is called "Niew Hollant," (after Hudson); and on another still, the shore between Race Point and Wood End appears to be called "Bevechier." In Champlain's admirable Map of New France, including the oldest recognizable map of what is now the New England coast with which I am acquainted, Cape Cod is called C. Blan (i.e. Cape White), from the color of its sands, and Massachusetts Bay is Baye Blanche. It was visited by De Monts and Champlain in 1605, and the next year was further explored by Poitrincourt and Champlain. The latter has given a particular account of these explorations in his "Voyages," together with separate charts and soundings of two of its harbors,—*Malle Barre*, the Bad Bar (Nauset Harbor?), a name now applied to what the French called *Cap Baturier*, and *Port Fortune*, apparently Chatham Harbor. Both these names are copied on the map of "Novi Belgii," in Ogilvy's America. He also describes minutely the manners and customs of the savages, and represents by a plate the savages surprising the French and killing five or six of them. The French afterward killed some of the natives, and wished, by way of revenge, to carry off some and make them grind in their hand-mill at Port Royal.

It is remarkable that there is not in English any adequate or correct account of the French exploration of what is now the coast of New England, between 1604 and 1608, though it is conceded that they then made the first permanent European settlement on the continent of North America north of St. Augustine. If the lions had been the painters it would have been otherwise. This omission is probably to be accounted for partly by the fact that the *early edition* of Champlain's "Voyages" had not been consulted for this purpose. This contains by far the most particular, and, I think, the most interesting chapter of what we may call the Ante-Pilgrim history of New England, extending to one hundred and sixty pages quarto; but appears to be unknown equally to the historian and the orator on Plymouth Rock. Bancroft does not mention Champlain at all among the authorities for De Monts's expedition, nor does he say that he ever visited the coast of New England. Though he bore the title of pilot to De Monts, he was, in *another sense*, the leading spirit, as well as the historian of the expedition. Holmes, Hildreth, and Barry, and apparently all our historians who mention Champlain, refer to the edition of 1632, in which all the separate charts of our harbors, etc., and about one-half the narrative, are omitted; for the author explored so many lands afterward that he could afford to forget a part of what he had done. Hildreth, speaking of De Monts's expedition, says that "he looked into the Penobscot [in 1605], which Pring had discovered two years before," saying nothing about Champlain's extensive exploration of it for De Monts in 1604 (Holmes says 1608, and refers to Purchas); also that he followed in the track of Pring along the coast "to Cape Cod, which he called Malabarre." (Haliburton had made the same statement before him in 1829. He called it Cap Blanc, and Malle Barre (the Bad Bar) was the name given to a harbor on the east side of the Cape). Pring says nothing about a river there. Belknap says that Weymouth discovered it in 1605. Sir F. Gorges, says, in his narration (Maine Hist. Coll., Vol. II., p. 19), 1658, that Pring in 1606 "made a perfect discovery of all the rivers and harbors." This is the most I can find. Bancroft makes Champlain to have dis-covered more western rivers in Maine, not naming the Penobscot; he, however, must have been the discoverer of distances on this river (see Belknap, p. 147). Pring was absent from England only about six months, and sailed by this part of Cape Cod (Malabarre) be-cause it yielded no sassafras, while the French, who probably had not heard of Pring, were patiently for years exploring the coast in search of a place of settlement, sounding and surveying its harbors.

John Smith's map, published in 1616, from observations in 1614-15, is by many regarded as the oldest map of New England. It is the first that was made after this country was called New England, for he so called it; but in Champlain's "Voyages," edition 1613 (and Lescarbot, in 1612, quotes a still earlier account of his voyage), there is a map of it made when it was known to Christendom as New France, called *Carte Géographique de la Nouvelle Franse faictte par le Sieur de Champlain Saint Tongois Cappitaine ordinaire pour le roi en la Marine,—faict l'en 1612*, from his observations between 1604 and 1607; a map extending from Labrador to Cape Cod and westward *to the Great Lakes*, and crowded with information, geographical, ethnographical, zoölogical, and botanical. He even gives the variation of the compass as observed by himself at that date on many parts of the coast. This, taken together with the many *separate charts* of harbors and their soundings on a large scale, which this volume contains,—among the rest. *Qui ni be quy* (Kennebec), *Chouacoit R.* (Saco R.), *Le Beau port, Port St. Louis* (near Cape Ann), and others on our coast,—but *which are not in the edition of 1632*, makes this a completer map of the New England and adjacent northern coast than was made for half a century afterward, almost, we might be allowed to say, till another Frenchman, Des Barres, made another for us, which only our late Coast Survey has superseded. Most of the maps of this coast made for a long time after betray their indebtedness to Champlain. He was a skilful navigator, a man of science, and geographer to the King of France. He crossed the Atlantic about twenty times, and made nothing of it; often in a small vessel in which few would dare to go to sea today; and on one occasion making the voyage from Tadoussac to St. Malo in eighteen days. He was in this neighborhood, that is, between Annapolis, Nova Scotia, and Cape Cod, observing the land and its inhabitants, and making a map of the coast, from May, 1604, to September, 1607, *or about three and a half years*, and he has described minutely his method of surveying harbors. By his own account, a part of his map was engraved in 1604 (?). When Pont-Gravé and others returned to France in 1606, he remained at Port Royal with Poitrincourt, "in order," says he, "by the aid of God, to finish the chart of the coasts which I had begun"; and again in his volume, printed before John Smith visited this part of America, he says: "It seems to me that I have done my duty as far as I could, if I have not forgotten to put in my said chart whatever I saw, and give a particular knowledge to the public of what had never been described nor discovered so particularly as I have done it, although some other may have heretofore written of it; but it was a very small affair in comparison with what we have discovered within the last ten years."

It is not generally remembered, if known, by the descendants of the Pilgrims, that when their forefathers were spending their first memorable winter in the New World, they had for neighbors a colony of French no further off than Port Royal (Annapolis, Nova Scotia), three hundred miles distant (Prince seems to make it about five hundred miles); where, in spite of many vicissitudes, they had been for fifteen years. They built a grist-mill there as early as 1606; also made bricks and turpentine on a stream, Williamson says, in 1606. De Monts, who was a Protestant, brought his minister with him, who came to blows with the Catholic priest on the subject of religion. Though these founders of Acadie endured no less than the Pilgrims, and about the same proportion of them—thirty-five out of seventy-nine (Williamson's Maine says thirty-six out of seventy)—died the first winter at St. Croix, 1604-5, sixteen years earlier, no orator, to my knowledge, has ever celebrated their enterprise (Williamson's History of Maine does considerably), while the trials which their successors and descendants endured at the hands of the English have furnished a theme for both the historian and poet. (See Bancroft's History and Longfellow's Evangeline.) The remains at their fort at St. Croix were discovered at the end of the last century, and helped decide where the true St. Croix, our boundary, was.

The very gravestones of those Frenchmen are probably older than the oldest English monument in New England north of the Elizabeth Islands, or perhaps anywhere in New England, for if there are any traces of Gosnold's storehouse left, his strong works are gone. Bancroft says, advisedly, in 1834, "It requires a believing eye to discern the ruins of the fort"; and that there were no ruins of a fort in 1837. Dr. Charles T. Jackson tells me that, in the course of a geological survey in 1827, he discovered a gravestone, a slab of trap rock, on Goat

Island, opposite Annapolis (Port Royal), in Nova Scotia, bearing a Masonic coat-of-arms and the date 1606, which is fourteen years earlier than the landing of the Pilgrims. This was left in the possession of Judge Haliburton, of Nova Scotia.

There were Jesuit priests in what has since been called New England, converting the savages at Mount Desert, then St. Savior, in 1613,—having come over to Port Royal in 1611, though they were almost immediately interrupted by the English, years before the Pilgrims came hither to enjoy their own religion. This according to Champlain. Charlevoix says the same; and after coming from France in 1611, went west from Port Royal along the coast, as far as the Kennebec in 1612, and was often carried from Port Royal to Mount Desert.

Indeed, the Englishman's history of *New* England commences only when it ceases to be *New* France. Though Cabot was the first to discover the continent of North America, Champlain, in the edition of his "Voyages" printed in 1632, after the English had for a season got possession of Quebec and Port Royal, complains with no little justice: "The common consent of all Europe is to represent New France as extending at least to the thirty-fifth and thirty-sixth degrees of latitude, as appears by the maps of the world printed in Spain, Italy, Holland, Flanders, Germany, and England, until they possessed themselves of the coasts of New France, where are Acadie, the Etchemins (Maine and New Brunswick), the Almouchicois (Massachusetts?), and the Great River St. Lawrence, where they have imposed, according to their fancy, such names as New England, Scotland, and others; but it is not easy to efface the memory of a thing which is known to all Christendom."

That Cabot merely landed on the uninhabitable shore of Labrador, gave the English no just title to New England, or to the United States, generally, any more than to Patagonia. His careful biographer (Biddle) is not certain in what voyage he ran down the coast of the United States as is reported, and no one tells us what he saw. Miller, in the New York Hist. Coll., Vol. I., p. 28, says he does not appear to have landed anywhere. Contrast with this Verrazzani's tarrying fifteen days at one place on the New England coast, and making frequent excursions into the interior thence. It chances that the latter's letter to Francis I., in 1524, contains "the earliest original account extant of the Atlantic coast of the United States"; and even from that time the northern part of it began to be called *La Terra Francese*, or French Land. A part of it was called New Holland before it was called New England. The English were very back-ward to explore and settle the continent which they had stumbled upon. The French preceded them both in their attempts to colonize the continent of North America (Carolina and Florida, 1562-4), and in their first permanent settlement (Port Royal, 1605); and the right of possession, naturally enough, was the one which England mainly respected and recognized in the case of Spain, of Portugal, and also of France, from the time of Henry VII.

The explorations of the French gave to the world the first valuable maps of these coasts. Denys of Honfleur made a map of the Gulf of St. Lawrence in 1506. No sooner had Cartier explored the St. Lawrence, in 1535, than there began to be published by his countrymen remarkably accurate charts of that river as far up as Montreal. It is almost all of the continent north of Florida that you recognize on charts for more than a generation afterward,—though Verrazzani's rude plot (made under French auspices) was regarded by Hackluyt, more than fifty years after his voyage (in 1524), as the most accurate representation of our coast. The French trail is distinct. They went measuring and sounding, and when they got home had something to show for their voyages and explorations. There was no danger of their charts being lost, as Cabot's have been.

The most distinguished navigators of that day were Italians, or of Italian descent, and Portuguese. The French and Spaniards, though less advanced in the science of navigation than the former, possessed more imagination and spirit of adventure than the English, and were better fitted to be the explorers of a new continent even as late as 1751.

This spirit it was which so early carried the French to the Great Lakes and the Mississippi on the north, and the Spaniard to the same river on the south. It was long before our frontiers reached their settlements in the west, and a *voyageur* or *coureur de bois* is still our conductor there. Prairie is a French word, as Sierra is a Spanish one. Augustine in Florida, and Santa Fé in New Mexico [1582], both built by the Spaniards, are considered the oldest towns in the United States. Within the memory of the oldest man, the Anglo-Americans were confined between the Appalachian Mountains and the sea, "a space not two hundred miles broad," while the Mississippi was by treaty the eastern boundary of New France. (See the pamphlet on settling the Ohio, London, 1763, bound up with the travels of Sir John Bartram.) So far as inland discovery was concerned, the adventurous spirit of the English was that of sailors who land but for a day, and their enterprise the enterprise of traders. Cabot spoke like an Englishman, as he was, if he said, as one reports, in reference to the discovery of the American Continent, when he found it running toward the north, that it was a great disappointment to him, being in his way to India; but we would rather add to than detract from the fame of so great a discoverer.

Samuel Penhallow, in his history (Boston, 1726), p. 51, speaking of "Port Royal and Nova Scotia," says of the last that its "first seizure was by Sir Sebastian Cobbet for the crown of Great Britain, in the reign of King Henry VII.; but lay dormant till the year 1621," when Sir William Alexander got a patent of it, and possessed it some years; and afterward Sir David Kirk was proprietor of it, but erelong, "to the surprise of all thinking men, it was given up unto the French."

Even as late as 1633 we find Winthrop, the first Governor of the Massachusetts Colony, who was not the most likely to be misinformed, who, moreover, has the *fame*, at least, of having discovered Wachusett Mountain (discerned it forty miles inland), talking about the "Great Lake" and the "hideous swamps about it," near which the Connecticut and the "Potomack" took their rise; and among the memorable events of the year 1642 he chronicles Darby Field, an Irishman's expedition to the "White hill," from whose top he saw eastward what he "judged to be the Gulf of Canada," and westward what he "judged to be the great lake which Canada River comes out of," and where he found much "Muscovy glass," and "could rive out pieces of forty feet long and seven or eight broad." While the very inhabitants of New England were thus fabling about the country a hundred miles inland, which was a *terra incognita* to them,—or rather many years before the earliest date referred to,—Champlain, the *first Governor of Canada*, not to mention the inland discoveries of Cartier,[1] Roberval, and others, of the preceding century, and his own earlier voyage, had already gone to war against the Iroquois in their forest forts, and penetrated to the Great Lakes and wintered there, before a Pilgrim had heard of New England.

In Champlain's "Voyages," printed in 1613, there is a plate representing a fight in which he aided the Canada Indians against the Iroquois, near the south end of Lake Champlain, in July, 1609, eleven years before the settlement of Plymouth. Bancroft says he joined the Algonquins in an expedition against the Iroquois, or Five Nations, in the northwest of New York. This is that "Great Lake," which the English, hearing some rumor of from the French, long after, locate in an "Imaginary Province called Laconia, and spent several years about 1630 in the vain attempt to discover." (Sir Ferdinand Gorges, in Maine Hist. Coll., Vol. II., p. 68.) Thomas Morton has a chapter on this "Great Lake." In the edition of Champlain's map dated 1632, the Falls of Niagara appear; and in a great lake northwest of *Mer Douce* (Lake Huron) there is an island represented, over which is written, "*Isle ou il y a une mine de cuivre*,"—"Island where there is a mine of copper." This will do for an offset to our Governor's "Muscovy Glass." Of all these adventures and discoveries we have a minute and faithful account, giving facts and dates as well as charts and soundings, all scientific and Frenchman-like, with scarcely one fable or traveller's story.

Probably Cape Cod was visited by Europeans long before the seventeenth century. It may be that Cabot himself beheld it. Verrazzani, in 1524, according to his own account, spent fifteen days on our coast, in latitude 41° 40 minutes (some suppose in the harbor of Newport), and often went five or six leagues into the interior there, and he says that he sailed thence at once one hundred and fifty leagues northeasterly, *always in sight of the coast*. There is a chart in Hackluyt's "Divers Voyages," made according to Verrazzani's plot, which last is praised for its accuracy by Hackluyt, but I cannot distinguish Cape Cod on it, unless it is the "C. Arenas," which is in the right latitude, though ten degrees west of "Claudia," which is thought to be Block Island.

The "Biographic Universelle" informs us that "An ancient manuscript chart drawn in 1529 by Diego Ribeiro, a Spanish cosmographer, has preserved the memory of the voyage of Gomez [a Portuguese sent out by Charles the Fifth]. One reads in it under (*au dessous*) the place occupied by the States of New York, Connecticut, and Rhode Island, *Terre d'Etienne Gomez, qu'il découvrit en* 1525 (Land of Etienne Gomez, which he discovered in 1525)." This chart, with a memoir, was published at Weimar in the last century.

Jean Alphonse, Roberval's pilot in Canada in 1642, one of the most skilful navigators of his time, and who has given remarkably minute and accurate direction for sailing up the St. Lawrence, showing that he knows what he is talking about, says in his "*Routier*" (it is in Hackluyt), "I have been at a bay as far as the forty-second degree, between Norimbegue [the Penobscot?] and Florida, but I have not explored the bottom of it, and I do not know whether it passes from one land to the other," *i.e.* to Asia. (" J'ai été à une Baye jusques par les 42ᵉ degres entre la Norimbegue et la Floride; mais je n'en ai pas cherché le fond, et ne sçais pas si elle passe d'une terre à l'autre.") This may refer to Massachusetts Bay, if not possibly to the western inclination of the coast a little farther south. When he says, "I have no doubt that the Norimbegue enters into the river of Canada," he is perhaps so interpreting some account which the Indians had given respecting the route from the St. Lawrence to the Atlantic by the St. John, or Penobscot, or possibly even the Hudson River.

We hear rumors of this country of "Norumbega" and its great city from many quarters. In a discourse by a great French sea-captain in Ramusio's third volume (1556-65), this is said to be the name given to the land by its inhabitants, and Verrazzani is called the discoverer of it; another in 1607 makes the natives call it, or the river, Aguncia. It is represented as an island on an accompanying chart. It is frequently spoken of by old writers as a country of indefinite extent, between Canada and Florida, and it appears as a large island with Cape Breton at its eastern extremity, on the map made according to Verrazzani's plot in Hackluyt's "Divers Voyages." These maps and rumors may have been the origin of the notion, common among the early settlers, that

New England was an island. The country and city of Norumbega appear about where Maine now is on a map in Ortelius ("Theatrum Orbis Terrarum," Antwerp, 1570), and the "R. Grande" is drawn where the Penobscot or St. John might be.

In 1604, Champlain being sent by the Sieur de Monts to explore the coast of Norumbegue, sailed up the Penobscot twenty-two or twenty-three leagues from "Isle Haute," or till he was stopped by the falls. He says: "I think that this river is that which many pilots and historians call Norumbegue, and which the greater part have described as great and spacious, with numerous islands; and its entrance in the forty-third or forty-third and one half or, according to others, the forty-fourth degree of latitude, more or less." He is convinced that "the greater part" of those who speak of a great city there have never seen it, but repeat a mere rumor, but he thinks that some have seen the mouth of the river since it answers to their description.

Under date of 1607 Champlain writes: "Three or four leagues north of the Cap de Poitrincourt [near the head of the Bay of Fundy in Nova Scotia] we found a cross, which was very old, covered with moss and almost all decayed, which was an evident sign that there had formerly been Christians there."

Also the following passage from Lescarbot will show how much the neighboring coasts were frequented by Europeans in the sixteenth century. Speaking of his return from Port Royal to France in 1607, he says: "At last, within four leagues of Campseau [the Gut of Canso], we arrived at a harbor [in Nova Scotia], where a worthy old gentleman from St. John de Lus, named Captain Savale, was fishing, who received us with the utmost courtesy. And as this harbor, which is small, but very good, has no name, I have given it on my geographical chart the name of Savalet. [It is on Champlain's map also.] This worthy man told us that this voyage was the forty-second which he had made to those parts, and yet the Newfoundlanders [*Terre neuviers*] make only one a year. He was wonderfully content with his fishery, and informed us that he made daily fifty crowns' worth of cod, and that his voyage would be worth ten thousand francs. He had sixteen men in his employ; and his vessel was of eighty tons, which could carry a hundred thousand dry cod." (Histoire de la Nouvelle France, 1612.) They dried their fish on the rocks on shore.

The "Isola della Réna" (Sable Island?) appears on the chart of "Nuova Francia" and Norumbega, accompanying the "Discourse" above referred to in Ramusio's third volume, edition 1556-65. Champlain speaks of there being at the Isle of Sable, in 1604, "grass pastured by oxen (*bœufs*) and cows which the Portuguese carried there more than sixty years ago," *i.e.* sixty years before 1613; in a later edition he says, which came out of a Spanish vessel which was lost in endeavoring to settle on the Isle of Sable; and he states that De la Roche's men, who were left on this island seven years from 1598, lived on the flesh of these cattle which they found "*en quantie)*," and built houses out of the wrecks of vessels which came to the island ("perhaps Gilbert's"), there being no wood or stone. Lescarbot says that they lived "on fish and the milk of cows left there about eighty years before by Baron de Leri and Saint Just." Charlevoix says they ate up the cattle and then lived on fish. Haliburton speaks of cattle left there as a rumor. De Leri and Saint Just had suggested plans of colonization on the Isle of Sable as early as 1515 (1508?) according to Bancroft, referring to Charlevoix. These are but a few of the instances which I might quote.

Cape Cod is commonly said to have been discovered in 1602. We will consider at length under what circumstances, and with what observation and expectations, the first Englishmen whom history clearly discerns approached the coast of New England. According to the accounts of Archer and Brereton (both of whom accompanied Gosnold), on the 26th of March, 1602, old style. Captain Bartholomew Gosnold set sail from Falmouth, England, for the North part of Virginia, in a small bark called the *Concord*, they being in all, says one account, "thirty-two persons, whereof eight mariners and sailors, twelve purposing upon the discovery to return with the ship for England, the rest remain there for population." This is regarded as "the first attempt of the English to make a settlement within the limits of New England." Pursuing a new and a shorter course than the usual one by the Canaries, "the 14th of April following" they had sight of Saint Mary's, an island of the Azores. As their sailors were few and "none of the best" (I use their own phrases), and they were "going upon an unknown coast," they were not "overbold to stand in with the shore but in open weather"; so they made their first discovery of land with the lead. The 23d of April the ocean appeared yellow, but on taking up some of the water in a bucket, "it altered not either in color or taste from the sea azure." The 7th of May they saw divers birds whose names they knew, and many others in their "English tongue of no name." The 8th of May "the water changed to a yellowish green, where at seventy fathoms" they "had ground." The 9th, they had upon their lead "many glittering stones,"—"which might promise some mineral matter in the bottom." The 10th, they were over a bank which they thought to be near the western end of St. John's Island, and saw schools of fish. The 12th, they say, "continually passed fleeting by us sea-oare, which seemed to have their movable course towards the northeast." On the 13th, they observed "great beds of weeds, much wood, and divers things else floating by," and "had smelling of the shore much as from the southern Cape and Andalusia in Spain." On Friday, the 14th, early in the morning they descried land on the north, in the latitude of forty-three degrees, apparently some part of the coast of Maine. Williamson (History of Maine) says it certainly could not have been south of the central Isle of Shoals. Belknap inclines to think it the south side of Cape Ann. Standing fair along by the shore, about twelve o'clock the same day, they came to anchor and were visited by eight savages, who came off to them "in a Biscay shallop, with sail and oars,"—"an iron grapple, and a kettle of copper." These they at first mistook for "Christians distressed." One of them was "apparelled with a waistcoat and breeches of black serge, made after our sea-fashion, hoes and shoes on his feet; all the rest (saving one that had a pair of breeches of blue cloth) were naked." They appeared to have had dealings with "some Basques of St. John de Luz, and to understand much more than we," say the English, "for want of language, could comprehend." But they soon "set sail westward, leaving them and their coast." (This was a remarkable discovery for discoverers.)

"The 15th day," writes Gabriel Archer, "we had again sight of the land, which made ahead, being as we thought an island, by reason of a large sound that appeared westward between it and the main, for coming to the west end thereof, we did perceive a large opening, we called it Shoal Hope. Near this cape we came to anchor in fifteen fathoms, where we took great store of cod-fish, for which we altered the name and called it Cape Cod. Here we saw skulls of her-ring, mackerel, and other small fish, in great abundance. This is a low sandy shoal, but without danger; also we came to anchor again in sixteen fathoms, fair by the land in the latitude of forty-two degrees. This Cape is well near a mile broad, and lieth northeast by east. The captain went here ashore, and found the ground to be full of peas, strawberries, whortleberries, etc., as then unripe, the sand also by the shore somewhat deep; the firewood there by us taken in was of cypress, birch, witch-hazel, and beach. A young Indian came here to the captain, armed with his bow and arrows, and had certain plates of copper hanging at his ears; he showed a willingness to help us in our occasions."

"The 16th we trended the coast southerly, which was all champaign and full of grass, but the islands somewhat woody."

Or, according to the account of John Brereton, "riding here," that is, where they first communicated with the natives, "in no very good harbor, and withal doubting the weather, about three of the clock the same day in the afternoon we weighed, and standing southerly off into sea the rest of that day and the night following, with a fresh gale of wind, in the morning we found ourselves embayed with a mighty headland; but coming to an anchor about nine of the clock the same day, within a league of the shore, we hoisted out the one half of our shallop, and Captain Bartholomew Gosnold, myself and three others, went ashore, being a white sandy and very bold shore; and marching all that afternoon with our muskets on our necks, on the highest hills which we saw (the weather very hot), at length we perceived this headland to be parcel of the main, and sundry islands lying almost round about it; so returning towards evening to our shallop (for by that time the other part was brought ashore and set together), we espied an Indian, a young man of proper stature, and of a pleasing countenance, and after some familiarity with him, we left him at the sea side, and returned to our ship, where in five or six hours' absence we had pestered our ship so with codfish, that we threw numbers of them overboard again; and surely I am persuaded that in the months of March, April, and May, there is upon this coast better fishing, and in as great plenty, as in Newfoundland; for the skulls of mackerel, herrings, cod, and other fish, that we daily saw as we went and came from the shore, were wonderful," etc.

"From this place we sailed round about this headland, almost all the points of the compass, the shore very bold; but as no coast is free from dangers, so I am persuaded this is as free as any. The land somewhat low, full of goodly woods, but in some places plain."

It is not quite clear on which side of the Cape they landed. If it was inside, as would appear from Brereton's words, "From this place we sailed round about this headland almost all the points of the compass," it must have been on the western shore either of Truro or Wellfleet. To one sailing south into Barnstable Bay along the Cape, the only "white, sandy, and very bold shore" that appears is in these towns, though the bank is not so high there as on the eastern side. At a distance of four or five miles the sandy cliffs there look like a long fort of yellow sandstone, they are so level and regular, especially in Wellfleet,—the fort of the land defending itself against the encroachments of the Ocean. They are streaked here and there with a reddish sand as if painted. Farther south the shore is more flat, and less *obviously* and abruptly sandy, and a little tinge of green here and there in the marshes appears to the sailor like a rare and precious emerald. But in the Journal of Pring's Voyage the next year (and Salterne, who was with Pring, had accompanied Gosnold) it is said, "Departing hence [*i.e.* from Savage Rocks] we bore unto that great gulf which Captain Gosnold overshot the year before."[2]

So they sailed round the Cape, calling the southeasterly extremity "Point Cave," till they came to an island which they named Martha's Vineyard (now called No Man's Land), and another on which they dwelt awhile, which they named Elizabeth's Island, in honor of the Queen, one of the group since so called, now known by its Indian name Cuttyhunk. There they built a small storehouse, the first house built by the English in New England, whose cellar could recently still be seen, made partly of stones taken from the beach. Bancroft says (edition of 1837), the ruins of the fort can no longer be discerned. They who were to have remained becoming discontented, all together set sail for England with a load of sassafras and other commodities, on the 18th of June following.

The next year came Martin Pring, looking for sassafras, and thereafter they began to come thick and fast, until long after sassafras had lost its reputation.

These are the oldest acounts which we have of Cape Cod, unless, perchance. Cape Cod is, as some suppose, the same with that "Kial-ar-nes" or Keel-Cape, on which, according to old Icelandic manuscripts, Thorwald, son of Eric the Red, after sailing many days southwest from Greenland, broke his keel in the year 1004; and where, according to another, in some respects less trustworthy manuscript, Thor-finn Karlsefue ("that is, one who promises or is destined to be an able or great man"; he is said to have had a son born in New. England, from whom Thorwaldsen the sculptor was descended), sailing past, in the year 1007, with his wife Gudrida, Snorre Thorbrandson, Biarne Grinolfson, and Thorhall Garnlason, distinguished Norsemen, in three ships containing "one hundred and sixty men and all sorts of live stock" (probably the first Norway rats among the rest), having the land "on the right side" of them, "roved ashore," and found "*ör-æfi* (trackless deserts)," and "*Strand-ir láng-ar ok sand-ar* (long narrow beaches and sand-hills)," and "called the shores *Furdustrand-ir* (Wonder-Strands), because the sailing by them seemed long."

According to the Icelandic manuscripts, *Thorwald* was the first, then,—unless possibly one Biarne Heriulfson (*i.e.* son of Heriulf) who had been seized with a great desire to travel, sailing from Iceland to Greenland in the year 986 to join his father who had migrated thither, for he had resolved, says the manuscript, "to spend the following winter, like all the preceding ones, with his father,"—being driven far to the southwest by a storm, when it cleared up saw the low land of Cape Cod looming faintly in the distance; but this not answering to the description of Greenland, he put his vessel about, and, sailing northward along the coast, at length reached Greenland and his father. At any rate, he may put forth a strong claim to be regarded as the discoverer of the American continent.

These Northmen were a hardy race, whose younger sons inherited the ocean, and traversed it without chart or compass, and they are said to have been "the first who learned the art of sailing on a wind." Moreover, they had a habit of casting their door-posts overboard and settling wherever they went ashore. But as Biarne, and Thorwald, and Thorfinn have not mentioned the latitude and longitude distinctly enough, though we have great respect for them as skilful and adventurous navigators, we must for the present remain in doubt as to what capes they did see. We think that they were considerably further north.

If time and space permitted, I could present the claims of other several worthy persons. Lescarbot, in 1609, asserts that the French sailors had been accustomed to frequent the Newfoundland Banks from time immemorial, "for the codfish with which they feed almost all Europe and supply all sea-going vessels," and accordingly "the language of the nearest lands is half Basque"; and he quotes Postel, a learned but extravagant French author, born in 1510, only six years after the Basques, Bretons, and Normans are said to have discovered the Grand Bank and adjacent islands, as saying, in his *Charte Géographique*, which we have not seen: "Terra haec ob lucrosissimam piscationis utilitatem summa litterarum memoria a Gallis adiri solita, et ante mille sexcentos annos frequentari solita est; sed eo quod sit urbibus inculta et vasta, spreta est." "This land, on account of its very lucrative fishery, was accustomed to be visited by the Gauls from the very dawn of history, and more than sixteen hundred years ago was accustomed to be frequented; but because it was unadorned with cities, and waste, it was despised."

It is the old story. Bob Smith discovered the mine, but I discovered it to the world. And now Bob Smith is putting in his claim.

But let us not laugh at Postel and his visions. He was perhaps better posted up than we; and if he does seem to draw the long bow, it may be because he had a long way to shoot,—quite across the Atlantic, If

America was found and lost again once, as most of us believe, then why not twice? especially as there were likely to be so few records of an earlier discovery. Consider what stuff history is made of,—that for the most part it is merely a story agreed on by posterity. Who will tell us even how many Russians were engaged in the battle of the Chernaya, the other day? Yet no doubt, Mr. Scriblerus, the historian, will fix on a definite number for the schoolboys to commit to their excellent memories. What, then, of the number of Persians at Salamis? The historian whom I read knew as much about the position of the parties and their tactics in the last-mentioned affair, as they who describe a recent battle in an article for the press now-a-days, before the particulars have arrived. I believe that, if I were to live the life of mankind over again myself (which I would not be hired to do), with the Universal History in my hands, I should not be able to tell what was what.

Earlier than the date Postel refers to, at any rate. Cape Cod lay in utter darkness to the civilized world, though even then the sun rose from eastward out of the sea every day, and, rolling over the Cape, went down westward into the Bay. It was even then Cape and Bay,—ay, the Cape of *Codfish*, and the Bay of the *Massachusetts*, perchance.

Quite recently, on the 11th of November, 1620, old style, as is well known, the Pilgrims in the *Mayflower* came to anchor in Cape Cod harbor. They had loosed from Plymouth, England, the 6th of September, and, in the words of "Mourts' Relation," "after many difficulties in boisterous storms, at length, by God's providence, upon the 9th of November, we espied land, which we deemed to be Cape Cod, and so afterward it proved. Upon the 11th of November we came to anchor in the bay, which is a good harbor and pleasant bay, circled round except in the entrance, which is about four miles over from land to land, compassed about to the very sea with oaks, pines, juniper, sassafras, and other sweet wood. It is a harbor wherein a thousand sail of ships may safely ride. There we relieved ourselves with wood and water, and refreshed our people, while our shallop was fitted to coast the bay, to search for an habitation." There we put up at Fuller's Hotel, passing by the Pilgrim House as too high for us (we learned afterward that we need not have been so particular), and we refreshed ourselves with hashed fish and beans, beside taking in a supply of liquids (which were not intoxicating), while our legs were refitted to coast the backside. Further say the Pilgrims: "We could not come near the shore by three quarters of an English mile, because of shallow water; which was a great prejudice to us; for our people going on shore were forced to wade a bow-shot or two in going aland, which caused many to get colds and coughs; for it was many times freezing cold weather." They afterwards say: "It brought much weakness amongst us"; and no doubt it led to the death of some at Plymouth.

The harbor of Provincetown is very shallow near the shore, especially about the head, where the Pilgrims landed. When I left this place the next summer, the steamer could not get up to the wharf, but we were carried out to a large boat in a cart as much as thirty rods in shallow water, while a troop of little boys kept us company, wading around, and thence we pulled to the steamer by a rope. The harbor being thus shallow and sandy about the shore, coasters are accustomed to run in here to paint their vessels, which are left high and dry when the tide goes down.

It chanced that the Sunday morning that we were there, I had joined a party of men who were smoking and lolling over a pile of boards on one of the wharves (*nihil humanum a me, etc.*), when our landlord, who was a sort of tithing-man, went off to stop some sailors who were engaged in painting their vessel. Our party was recruited from time to time by other citizens, who came rubbing their eyes as if they had just got out of bed; and one old man remarked to me that it was the custom there to lie abed very late on Sunday, it being a day of rest. I remarked that, as I thought, they might as well let the men paint, for all us. It was not noisy work, and would not disturb our devotions. But a young man in the company, taking his pipe out of his mouth, said that it was a plain contradiction of the law of God, which he quoted, and if they did not have some such regulation, vessels would run in there to tar, and rig, and paint, and they would have no Sabbath at all. This was a good argument enough, if he had not put it in the name of religion. The next summer, as I sat on a hill there one sultry Sunday afternoon the meeting-house windows being open, my meditations were interrupted by the noise of a preacher who shouted like a boatswain, profaning the quiet atmosphere, and who, I fancied, must have taken off his coat. Few things could have been more disgusting or disheartening. I wished the tithing-man would stop him.

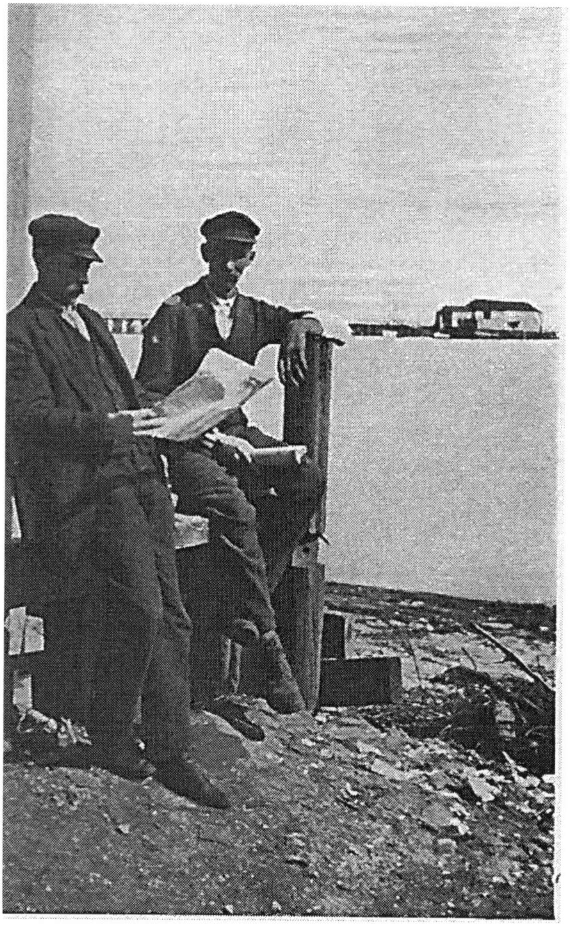

## The day of rest

The Pilgrims say: "There was the greatest store of fowl that ever we saw."

We saw no fowl there, except gulls of various kinds; but the greatest store of them that ever we saw was on a flat but slightly covered with water on the east side of the harbor, and we observed a man who had landed there from a boat creeping along the shore in order to get a shot at them, but they all rose and flew away in a great scattering flock, too soon for him, having apparently got their dinners, though he did not get his.

It is remarkable that the Pilgrims (or their reporter) describe this part of the Cape, not only as well wooded, but as having a deep and excellent soil, and hardly mention the word *sand*. Now what strikes the voyager is the barrenness and desolation of the land. *They* found "the ground or earth sand-hills, much like the downs in Holland, but much better the crust of the earth, a spit's depth, excellent black earth." *We* found that the earth had lost its crust,—if, in-deed, it ever had any,— and that there was no soil to speak of. We did not see enough black earth in Provincetown to fill a flower-pot, unless in the swamps. They found it "all wooded with oaks, pines, sassafras, juniper, birch, holly, vines, some ash, walnut; the wood for the most part open and without underwood, fit either to go or ride in." We saw scarcely anything high enough to be called a tree, except a little low wood at the east end of the town, and the few ornamental trees in its yards,—only a few small specimens of some of the above kinds on the sand-hills in the rear; but it was all thick shrubbery, without any large wood above it, very unfit either to go or ride in. The greater part of the land was a perfect desert of yellow sand, rippled like waves by the wind, in which only a little Beach-grass grew here and there. They say that, just after passing the head of East Harbor Creek, the boughs and bushes "tore" their "very armor in pieces" (the same thing happened to such armor as we wore, when out of curiosity we took to the bushes); or they came to deep valleys, "full of brush, wood-gaile, and long grass," and "found springs of fresh water."

For the most part we saw neither bough nor bush, not so much as a shrub to tear our clothes against if we would, and a sheep would lose none of its fleece, even if it found herbage enough to make fleece grow there. We saw rather beach and poverty-grass, and merely sorrel enough to color the surface. I suppose, then, by Woodgaile they mean the Bay berry.

All accounts agree in affirming that this part of the Cape was *comparatively* well wooded a century ago. But notwithstanding the great changes which have taken place in these respects, I cannot but think that we must make some allowance for the greenness of the Pilgrims in these matters, which caused them to see green. We do not believe that the trees were large or the soil was deep here. Their account may be true particularly, but it is generally false. They saw literally, as well as figuratively, but one side of the Cape. They naturally exaggerated the fairness and attractiveness of the land, for they were glad to get to any land at all after that anxious voyage. Everything appeared to them of the color of the rose, and had the scent of juniper and sassafras. Very different is the general and off-hand account given by Captain John Smith, who was on this coast six years earlier, and speaks like an old traveller, voyager, and soldier, who had seen too much of the world to exaggerate, or even to dwell long, on a part of it. In his "Description of New England," printed in 1616, after speaking of Accomack, since called Plymouth, he says: "Cape Cod is the next presents itself, which is only a headland of high hills of sand, overgrown with shrubby pines, *hurts* [i.e. whorts, or whortleberries], and such trash, but an excellent harbor for all weathers. This Cape is made by the main sea on the one side, and a great bay on the other, in form of a sickle." Champlain had already written, "Which we named *Cap Blanc* (Cape White), because they were sands and downs (*sables et dunes*) which appeared thus."

When the Pilgrims get to Plymouth their reporter says again, "The land for the crust of the earth is a spit's depth,"—that would seem to be their recipe for an earth's crust,—"excellent black mould and fat in some places." However, according to Bradford himself, whom some consider the author of part of "Mourt's Relation," they who came over in the *Fortune* the next year were somewhat daunted when "they came into the harbor of Cape Cod, and there saw nothing but a naked and barren place." They soon found out their mistake with respect to the goodness of Plymouth soil. Yet when at length, some years later, when they were fully satisfied of the poorness of the place which they had chosen, "the greater part," says Bradford, "consented to a removal to a place called Nausett," they agreed to remove all together to Nauset, now Eastham, which was jumping out of the frying-pan into the fire; and some of the most respectable of the inhabitants of Plymouth did actually remove thither accordingly.

It must be confessed that the Pilgrims possessed but few of the qualities of the modern pioneer. They were not the ancestors of the American backwoodsmen. They did not go at once into the woods with their axes. They were a family and church, and were more anxious to keep together, though it were on the sand, than to explore and colonize a New World. When the above-mentioned company removed to Eastham, the church at Plymouth was left, to use Bradford's expression, "like an ancient mother grown old, and forsaken of her children." Though they landed on Clark's Island in Plymouth harbor, the 9th of December (O. S.), and the 16th all hands came to Plymouth, and the 18th they rambled about the mainland, and the 19th decided to settle there, it was the 8th of January before Francis Billington went with one of the master's mates to look at the magnificent pond or lake now called "Billington Sea," about two miles distant, which he had discovered from the top of a tree, and mistook for a great sea. And the 7th of March "Master Carver with five others went to the great ponds which seem to be excellent fishing," both which points are within the compass of an ordinary afternoon's ramble,—however wild the country. It is true they were busy at first about their building, and were hindered in that by much foul weather; but a party of emigrants to California or Oregon, with no less work on their hands,—and more hostile Indians,—would do as much exploring the first afternoon, and the Sieur de Champlain would have sought an interview with the savages, and examined the country as far as the Connecticut, and made a map of it, before Billington had climbed his tree. Or contrast them only with the French searching for copper about the Bay of Fundy in

1603, tracing up small streams with Indian guides. Nevertheless, the Pilgrims were pioneers and the ancestors of pioneers, in a far grander enterprise.

By this time we saw the little steamer *Naushon* entering the harbor, and heard the sound of her whistle, and came down from the hills to meet her at the wharf. So we took leave of Cape Cod and its inhabitants. We liked the manners of the last, what little we saw of them, very much. They were particularly downright and good-humored. The old people appeared remarkably well preserved, as if by the saltness of the atmosphere, and after having once mistaken, we could never be certain whether we were talking to a coeval of our grandparents, or to one of our own age. They are said to be more purely the descendants of the Pilgrims than the inhabitants of any other part of the State. We were told that "sometimes, when the court comes together at Barnstable, they have not a single criminal to try, and the jail is shut up." It was "to let" when we were there. Until quite recently there was no regular lawyer below Orleans. Who then will complain of a few regular man-eating sharks along the back-side?

One of the ministers of Truro, when I asked what the fishermen did in the winter, answered that they did nothing but go a-visiting, sit about and tell stories,—though they worked hard in summer. Yet it is not a long vacation they get. I am sorry that I have not been there in the winter to hear their yarns. Almost every Cape man is Captain of some craft or other,—every man at least who is at the head of his own affairs, though it is not every one that is, for some heads have the force of *Alpha privative*, negativing all the efforts which Nature would fain make through them. The greater number of men are merely corporals. It is worth the while to talk with one whom his neighbors address as Captain, though his craft may have long been sunk, and he may be holding by his teeth to the shattered mast of a pipe alone, and only gets half-seas-over in a figurative sense, now. He is pretty sure to vindicate his right to the title at last,—can tell one or two good stories at least.

For the most part we saw only the back-side of the towns, but our story is true as far as it goes. We might have made more of the Bay side, but we were inclined to open our eyes widest at the Atlantic. We did not care to see those features of the Cape in which it is inferior or merely equal to the mainland, but only those in which it is peculiar or superior. We cannot say how its towns look in front to one who goes to meet them; we went to see the ocean behind them. They were merely the raft on which we stood, and we took notice of the barnacles which adhered to it, and some carvings upon it.

Before we left the wharf we made the acquaintance of a passenger whom we had seen at the hotel. When we asked him which way he came to Provincetown, he answered that he was cast ashore at Wood End, Saturday night, in the same storm in which the *St. John* was wrecked. He had been at work as a carpenter in Maine, and took passage for Boston in a schooner laden with lumber. When the storm came up, they endeavored to get into Provincetown harbor. "It was dark and misty," said he, "and as we were steering for Long Point Light we suddenly saw the land near us,—for our compass was out of order,—varied several degrees [a mariner always casts the blame on his compass],—but there being a mist on shore, we thought it was farther off than it was, and so held on, and we immediately struck on the bar. Says the Captain, 'We are all lost.' Says I to the Captain, 'Now don't let her strike again this way; head her right on.' The Captain thought a moment, and then headed her on. The sea washed completely over us, and wellnigh took the breath out of my body. I held on to the running rigging, but I have learned to hold on to the standing rigging the next time." "Well, were there any drowned?" I asked. "No; we all got safe to a house at Wood End, at midnight, wet to our skins, and half frozen to death." He had apparently spent the time since playing checkers at the hotel, and was congratulating himself on having beaten a tall fellow-boarder at that game. "The vessel is to be sold at auction to-day," he added. (We had heard the sound of the crier's bell which advertised it.) "The Captain is rather down about it, but I tell him to cheer up and he will soon get another vessel."

At that moment the Captain called to him from the wharf. He looked like a man just from the country, with a cap made of a woodchuck's skin, and now that I had heard a part of his history, he appeared singularly destitute,—a Captain without any vessel, only a great-coat! and that perhaps a borrowed one! Not even a dog followed him; only his title stuck to him. I also saw one of the crew. They all had caps of the same pattern, and wore a subdued look, in addition to their naturally aquiline features, as if a breaker—a "comber"—had washed over them. As we passed Wood End, we noticed the pile of lumber on the shore which had made the cargo of their vessel.

About Long Point in the summer you commonly see them catching lobsters for the New York market, from small boats just off the shore, or rather, the lobsters catch themselves, for they cling to the netting on which the bait is placed of their own accord, and thus are drawn up. They sell them fresh for two cents apiece. Man needs to know but little more than a lobster in order to catch him in his traps. The mackerel fleet had been getting to sea, one after another, ever since midnight, and as we were leaving the Cape we passed near to many of them under sail, and got a nearer view than we had had;—half a dozen red-shirted men and boys, leaning over the rail to look at us, the skipper shouting back the number of barrels he had caught, in answer to our inquiry. All sailors pause to watch a steamer, and shout in welcome or derision. In one a large Newfoundland dog put his paws on the rail and stood up as high as any of them, and looked as wise. But the skipper, who did not wish to be seen no better employed than a dog, rapped him on the nose and sent him below. Such is human justice! I thought I could hear him making an effective appeal down there from human to divine justice. He must have had much the cleanest breast of the two.

A Provincetown fishing-vessel

Still, many a mile behind us across the Bay, we saw the white sails of the mackerel fishers hovering round Cape Cod, and when they were all hull-down, and the low extremity of the Cape was also down, their white sails still appeared on both sides of it, around where it had sunk, like a city on the ocean, proclaiming the rare qualities of Cape Cod Harbor. But before the extremity of the Cape had completely sunk, it appeared like a filmy sliver of land lying flat on the ocean, and later still a mere reflection of a sand-bar on the haze above. Its name suggests a homely truth, but it would be more poetic if it described the impression which it makes on the beholder. Some capes have peculiarly suggestive names. There is Cape Wrath, the northwest point of

Scotland, for instance; what a good name for a cape lying far away dark over the water under a lowering sky!

Mild as it was on shore this morning, the wind was cold and piercing on the water. Though it be the hottest day in July on land, and the voyage is to last but four hours, take your thickest clothes with you, for you are about to float over melted icebergs. When I left Boston in the steamboat on the 25th of June the next year, it was a quite warm day on shore. The passengers were dressed in their thinnest clothes, and at first sat under their umbrellas, but when we were fairly out on the Bay, such as had only their coats were suffering with the cold, and sought the shelter of the pilot's house and the warmth of the chimney. But when we approached the harbor of Provincetown, I was surprised to perceive what an influence that low and narrow strip of sand, only a mile or two in width, had over the temperature of the air for many miles around. We penetrated into a sultry atmosphere where our thin coats were once more in fashion, and found the inhabitants sweltering.

Leaving far on one side Manomet Point in Plymouth and the Scituate shore, after being out of sight of land for an hour or two, for it was rather hazy, we neared the Cohasset Rocks again at Minot's Ledge, and saw the great Tupelo-tree on the edge of Scituate, which lifts its dome, like an umbelliferous plant, high over the surrounding forest, and is conspicuous for many miles over land and water. Here was the new iron light-house, then unfinished, in the shape of an egg-shell painted red, and placed high on iron pillars, like the ovum of a sea monster floating on the waves,—destined to be phosphorescent. As we passed it at half-tide we saw the spray tossed up nearly to the shell. A man was to live in that egg-shell day and night, a mile from the shore. When I passed it the next summer it was finished and two men lived in it, and a light-house keeper said that they told him that in a recent gale it had rocked so as to shake the plates off the table. Think of making your bed thus in the crest of a breaker! To have the waves, like a pack of hungry wolves, eying you always, night and day, and from time to time making a spring at you, almost sure to have you at last. And not one of all those voyagers can come to your relief,—but when your light goes out, it will be a sign that the light of your life has gone out also.

What a place to compose a work on breakers! This light-house was the cynosure of all eyes. Every passenger watched it for half an hour at least; yet a colored cook belonging to the boat, whom I had seen come out of his quarters several times to empty his dishes over the side with a flourish, chancing to come out just as we were abreast of this light, and not more than forty rods from it, and were all gazing at it, as he drew back his arm, caught sight of it, and with surprise exclaimed, "What's that?" He had been employed on this boat for a year, and passed this light every weekday, but as he had never chanced to empty his dishes just at that point, had never seen it before. To look at lights was the pilot's business; he minded the kitchen fire. It suggested how little some who voyaged round the world could manage to see. You would almost as easily believe that there are men who never yet chanced to come out at the right time to see the sun. What avails it though a light be placed on the top of a hill, if you spend all your life directly under the hill? It might as well be under a bushel. This light-house, as is well known, was swept away in a storm in April, 1851, and the two men in it, and the next morning not a vestige of it was to be seen from the shore.

A Hull man told me that he helped set up a white-oak pole on Minot's Ledge some years before. It was fifteen inches in diameter, forty-one feet high, sunk four feet in the rock, and was secured by four guys,—but it stood only one year. Stone piled up cob-fashion near the same place stood eight years.

When I crossed the Bay in the *Melrose* in July, we hugged the Scituate shore as long as possible, in order to take advantage of the wind. Far out on the Bay (off this shore) we scared up a brood of young ducks, probably black ones, bred hereabouts, which the packet had frequently disturbed in her trips. A townsman, who was making the voyage for the first time, walked slowly round into the rear of the helmsman, when we were in the middle of the Bay, and looking out over the sea, before he sat down there, remarked with as much originality as was possible for one who used a borrowed expression, "This is a great country." He had been a timber merchant, and I afterwards saw him taking the diameter of the mainmast with his stick, and estimating its height. I returned from the same excursion in the *Olata*, a very handsome and swift-sailing yacht, which left Provincetown at the same time with two other packets, the *Melrose* and *Frolic*. At first there was scarcely a breath of air stirring, and we loitered about Long Point for an hour in company,—with our heads over the rail watching the great sand-circles and the fishes at the bottom in calm water fifteen feet deep. But after clearing the Cape we rigged a flying-jib, and, as the Captain had prophesied, soon showed our consorts our heels. There was a steamer six or eight miles northward, near the Cape, towing a large ship toward Boston. Its smoke stretched perfectly horizontal several miles over the sea, and by a sudden change in its direction, warned us of a change in the wind before we felt it. The steamer appeared very far from the ship, and some young men who had frequently used the Captain's glass, but did not suspect that the vessels were connected, expressed surprise that they kept about the same distance apart for so many hours. At which the Captain dryly remarked, that probably they would never get any nearer together. As long as the wind held we kept pace with the steamer, but at length it died away almost entirely, and the flying-jib did all the work. When we passed the light-boat at Minot's Ledge, the *Melrose* and *Frolic* were just visible ten miles astern.

Consider the islands bearing the names of all the saints, bristling with forts like chestnuts-burs, or *echinidæ*, yet the police will not let a couple of Irishmen have a private sparring-match on one of them, as it is a government monopoly; all the great seaports are in a boxing attitude, and you must sail prudently between two tiers of stony knuckles before you come to feel the warmth of their breasts.

The Bermudas are said to have been discovered by a Spanish ship of that name which was wrecked on them, "which till then," says Sir John Smith, "for six thousand years had been nameless." The English did not stumble upon them in their first voyages to Virginia; and the first Englishman who was ever there was wrecked on them in 1593. Smith says, "No place known hath better walls nor a broader ditch." Yet at the very first planting of them with some sixty persons, in 1612, the first Governor, the same year, "built and laid the foundation of eight or nine forts." To be ready, one would say, to entertain the first ship's company that should be next shipwrecked on to them. It would have been more sensible to have built as many "Charity-houses." These are the vexed Bermoothees.

Our great sails caught all the air there was, and our low and narrow hull caused the least possible friction. Coming up the harbor against the stream we swept by everything. Some young men returning from a fishing excursion came to the side of their smack, while we were thus steadily drawing by them, and, bowing, observed, with the best possible grace, "We give it up." Yet sometimes we were nearly at a standstill. The sailors watched (two) objects on the shore to ascertain whether we advanced or receded. In the harbor it was like the evening of a holiday. The Eastern steamboat passed us with music and a cheer, as if they were going to a ball, when they might be going to—Davy's locker.

I heard a boy telling the story of Nix's mate to some girls as we passed that spot. That was the name of a sailor hung there, he said.— "If I am guilty, this island will remain; but if I am innocent it will be washed away," and now it is all washed away!

Next (?) came the fort on George's Island. These are bungling contrivances: not our *fortes* but our *foibles*. Wolfe sailed by the strongest fort in North America in the dark, and took it.

I admired the skill with which the vessel was at last brought to her place in the dock, near the end of Long Wharf. It was candle-light, and my eyes could not distinguish the wharves jutting out towards us, but it appeared like an even line of shore densely crowded with shipping. You could not have guessed within a quarter of a mile of Long Wharf. Nevertheless, we were to be blown to a crevice amid them,—steering right into the maze. Down goes the mainsail, and only the jib draws us along. Now we are within four rods of the shipping, having already dodged several outsiders; but it is still only a maze of spars, and rigging, and hulls,—not a crack can be seen. Down goes the jib, but still we advance. The Captain stands aft with one hand on the tiller, and the other holding his night-glass,—his son stands on the bowsprit straining his eyes,—the passengers feel their hearts halfway to their mouths, expecting a crash. "Do you see any room there?" asks the Captain, quietly. He must make up his mind in five seconds, else he will carry away that vessel's bowsprit, or lose his own. "Yes, sir, here is a place for us"; and in three minutes more we are fast to the wharf in a little gap between two bigger vessels.

And now we were in Boston. Whoever has been down to the end of Long Wharf, and walked through Quincy Market, has seen Boston.

Boston, New York, Philadelphia, Charleston, New Orleans, and the rest, are the names of wharves projecting into the sea (surrounded by the shops and dwellings of the merchants), good places to take in and to discharge a cargo (to land the products of other climes and load the exports of our own). I see a great many barrels and fig-drums,—piles of wood for umbrella-sticks,—blocks of granite and ice,—great heaps of goods, and the means of packing and conveying them,—much wrapping-paper and twine,—many crates and hogsheads and trucks,—and that is Boston. The more barrels, the more Boston. The museums and scientific societies and libraries are accidental. They gather around the sands to save carting. The wharf-rats and customhouse officers, and broken-down poets, seeking a fortune amid the barrels. Their better or worse lyceums, and preachings, and doctorings, these, too, are accidental, and the malls of commons are always small potatoes. When I go to Boston, I naturally go straight through the city (taking the Market in my way), down to the end of Long Wharf, and look off, for I have no cousins in the back alleys,—and there I see a great many countrymen in their shirt-sleeves from Maine, and Pennsylvania, and all along shore and in shore, and some foreigners beside, loading and unloading and steering their teams about, as at a country fair.

When we reached Boston that October, I had a gill of Provincetown sand in my shoes, and at Concord there was still enough left to sand my pages for many a day; and I seemed to hear the sea roar, as if I lived in a shell, for a week afterward.

The places which I have described may seem strange and remote to my townsmen,—indeed, from Boston to Provincetown is twice as far as from England to France; yet step into the cars, and in six hours you may stand on those four planks, and see the Cape which Gosnold is said to have discovered, and which I have so poorly described. If you had started when I first advised you, you might have seen our tracks in the sand, still fresh, and reaching all the way from the Nauset Lights to Race Point, some thirty miles,—for at every step we made an impression on the Cape, though we were not aware of it, and though our account may have made no impression on your minds. But what is our account? In it there is no roar, no beach-birds, no tow-cloth.

We often love to think now of the life of men on beaches,—at least in midsummer, when the weather is serene; their sunny lives on the sand, amid the beach-grass and the bayberries, their companion a cow, their wealth a jag of driftwood or a few beach-plums, and their music the surf and the peep of the beach-bird.

We went to see the Ocean, and that is probably the best place of all our coast to go to. If you go by water, you may experience what it is to leave and to approach these shores; you may see the Stormy Petrel by the way, θαλασσοδρόμα, running over the sea, and if the weather is but a little thick, may lose sight of the land in mid-passage. I do not know where there is another beach in the Atlantic States, attached to the mainland, so long, and at the same time so straight, and completely uninterrupted by creeks or coves or fresh-water rivers or marshes; for though there may be clear places on the map, they would probably be found by the foot traveller to be intersected by creeks and marshes; certainly there is none where there is a double way, such as I have described, a beach and a bank, which at the same time shows you the land and the sea, and part of the time two seas. The Great South Beach of Long Island, which I have since visited, is longer still without an inlet, but it is literally a mere sand-bar, exposed, several miles from the Island, and not the edge of a continent wasting before the assaults of the Ocean. Though wild and desolate, as it wants the bold bank, it possesses but half the grandeur of Cape Cod in my eyes, nor is the imagination contented with its southern aspect. The only other beaches of great length on our Atlantic coast, which I have heard sailors speak of, are those of Barnegat on the Jersey shore, and Currituck between Virginia and North Carolina; but these, like the last, are low and narrow sandbars, lying off the coast, and separated from the mainland by lagoons. Besides, as you go farther south, the tides are feebler, and cease to add variety and grandeur to the shore. On the Pacific side of our country also no doubt there is good walking to be found; a recent writer and dweller there tells us that "the coast from Cape Disappointment (or the Columbia River) to Cape Flattery (at the Strait of Juan de Fuca) is nearly north and south, and can be travelled almost its entire length on a beautiful sand-beach," with the exception of two bays, four or five rivers, and a few points jutting into the sea. The common shell-fish found there seem to be often of corresponding types, if not identical species, with those of Cape Cod. The beach which I have described, however, is not hard enough for carriages, but must be explored on foot. When one carriage has passed along, a following one sinks deeper still in its rut. It has at present no name any more than fame. That portion south of Nauset Harbor is commonly called Chatham Beach. The part in Eastham is called Nauset Beach, and off Wellfleet and Truro the Back-side, or sometimes, perhaps, Cape Cod Beach. I think that part which extends without interruption from Nauset Harbor to Race Point should be called Cape Cod Beach, and do so speak of it.

One of the most attractive points for visitors is in the northeast part of Wellfleet, where accommodations (I mean for men and women of tolerable health and habits) could probably be had within half a mile of the sea-shore. It best combines the country and the seaside. Though the Ocean is out of sight, its faintest murmur is audible, and you have only to climb a hill to find yourself on its brink. It is but a step from the glassy surface of the Herring Ponds to the big Atlantic Pond where the waves never cease to break. Or perhaps the Highland Light in Truro may compete with this locality, for there, there is a more uninterrupted view of the Ocean and the Bay, and in the summer there is always some air stirring on the edge of the bank there, so that the inhabitants know not what hot weather is. As for the view, the keeper of the light, with one or more of his family, walks out to the edge of the bank after every meal to look off, just as if they had not lived there all their days. In short, it will wear well. And what picture will you substitute for that, upon your walls? But ladies cannot get down the bank there at present without the aid of a block and tackle.

Most persons visit the sea-side in warm weather, when fogs are frequent, and the atmosphere is wont to be thick, and the charm of the sea is to some extent lost. But I suspect that the fall is the best season, for then the atmosphere is more transparent, and it is a greater pleasure to look out over the sea. The clear and bracing air, and the storms of autumn and winter even, are necessary in order that we may get the impression which the sea is calculated to make. In October, when the weather is not intolerably cold, and the landscape wears its autumnal tints, such as, methinks, only a Cape Cod landscape ever wears, especially if you have a storm during your stay,—that I am convinced is the best time to visit this shore. In autumn, even in August, the thoughtful days begin, and we can walk anywhere with profit. Beside, an outward cold and dreariness, which make it necessary to seek shelter at night, lend a spirit of adventure to a walk.

The time must come when this coast will be a place of resort for those New-Englanders who really wish to visit the sea-side. At present it is wholly unknown to the fashionable world, and probably it will never be agreeable to them. If it is merely a ten-pin alley, or a circular railway, or an ocean of mint-julep, that the visitor is in search of,—if he thinks more of the wine than the brine, as I suspect some do at Newport,—I trust that for a long time he will be disappointed here. But this shore will never be more attractive than it is now. Such beaches as are fashionable are here made and unmade in a day, I may almost say, by the sea shifting its sands. Lynn and Nantasket! this bare and bended arm it is that makes the bay in which they lie so snugly. What are springs and waterfalls? Here is the spring of springs, the waterfall of waterfalls. A storm in the fall or winter is the time to visit it; a light-house or a fisherman's hut the true hotel. A man may stand there and put all America behind him.

> [1] It is remarkable that the first, if not the only, part of New England which Cartier saw was Vermont (he also saw the mountains of New York), from Montreal Mountain, in 1535, sixty-seven years before Gosnold saw Cape Cod. *If seeing*

*is discovering*,—and that is *all* that it is proved that Cabot knew of the coast of the United States,—then Cartier (to omit Verrazani and Gomez) was the discoverer of New England rather than Gosnold, who is commonly so styled.

[2] "Savage Rock," which some have supposed to be, from the name, the *Salvages*, a ledge about two miles off Rockland, Cape Ann, was probably the *Nubble*, a large, high rock near the shore, on the east side of York Harbor, Maine. The first land made by Gosnold is presumed by experienced navigators to be Cape Elizabeth, on the same coast. (See Babson's History of Gloucester, Massachusetts.)

The University Press, Cambridge, U. S. A.

# APPENDIX

# PLOT SUMMARY

"Cape Cod" by Henry David Thoreau is a non-fiction travelogue chronicling Thoreau's journey through Cape Cod in the early 1850s. The book is divided into ten chapters, each focusing on a different aspect of Thoreau's exploration of the region.

Thoreau begins his journey by describing the landscape and geography of Cape Cod, with its sandy shores, dunes, and marshes. He reflects on the unique character of the Cape and its relationship with the sea.

As Thoreau travels along the coast, he encounters various individuals, including fishermen, sailors, and farmers. He engages in conversations with them, learning about their way of life and their perspectives on the natural world.

Throughout the book, Thoreau observes the wildlife of Cape Cod, from the migratory birds that inhabit the beaches to the seals that frolic in the waters offshore. He marvels at the beauty and diversity of the region's flora and fauna.

Thoreau also reflects on the history and culture of Cape Cod, from its Native American inhabitants to its early European settlers. He explores the remnants of past civilizations, including abandoned settlements and lighthouses.

As Thoreau travels further along the coast, he contemplates the transient nature of life and the passage of time. He muses on the impermanence of human existence and the enduring power of the natural world.

In the final chapters of the book, Thoreau returns to his reflections on the sea and its timeless presence in the landscape of Cape Cod. He concludes with a meditation on the interconnectedness of all living things and the eternal cycle of life and death.

Overall, "Cape Cod" is a lyrical and introspective journey through one of America's most iconic landscapes, offering readers a glimpse into the beauty, history, and mystery of this unique region. Thoreau's prose invites readers to slow down, observe the world around them, and contemplate the deeper truths of existence.

# HISTORICAL CONTEXT

"Following the Equator" by Mark Twain was published in 1897, a time marked by significant global changes and transitions. The late 19th century was a period of rapid industrialization, colonial expansion, and social upheaval, shaping the historical context in which Twain's travelogue emerged:

1. **Imperialism and Colonialism:** The late 19th century saw the peak of European imperialism, with major powers such as Britain, France, and Germany expanding their empires through colonization. Twain's travels take place against this backdrop of colonial dominance, providing insights into the impact of imperialism on indigenous cultures and societies.

2. **Technological Advancements:** The late 19th century witnessed remarkable technological advancements that transformed transportation, communication, and industry. The steamship, railway, and telegraph revolutionized travel and trade, enabling Twain to embark on his global journey and communicate with distant parts of the world.

3. **Social and Cultural Shifts:** The late 19th century was a period of profound social and cultural change, marked by urbanization, immigration, and the rise of industrial capitalism. Twain's observations reflect the diversity and complexity of societies he encounters, as well as the tensions arising from rapid social transformations.

4. **Globalization of Trade and Commerce:** The late 19th century saw the expansion of global trade networks, facilitated by

advancements in transportation and communication. Twain's travels through ports and trading centers highlight the interconnectedness of the global economy and the exchange of goods, ideas, and cultures.

5. **Literary and Intellectual Movements:** Twain's work emerged during a period of literary and intellectual ferment, with movements such as realism and naturalism challenging traditional literary conventions. "Following the Equator" reflects these literary trends, blending vivid storytelling with keen observations and social commentary.

6. **Political Unrest and Conflict:** The late 19th century was also marked by political unrest, conflicts, and revolutions in various parts of the world. Twain's travels take him through regions experiencing political upheaval, offering glimpses into the struggles for independence, self-determination, and social justice.

In summary, the historical context of "Following the Equator" encompasses the complex dynamics of imperialism, industrialization, globalization, and social change that characterized the late 19th century. Twain's travelogue provides valuable insights into the global landscape of his time, while also offering timeless reflections on the human condition and the nature of travel and exploration.

# BIOGRAPHY

## Henry David Thoreau

American essayist, poet and practical philosopher, Henry David Thoreau was a New England Transcendentalist and author of the book 'Walden.'

Henry David Thoreau began writing nature poetry in the 1840s, with poet Ralph Waldo Emerson as a mentor and friend. In 1845 he began his famous two-year stay on Walden Pond, which he wrote about in his masterwork, Walden. He also became known for his beliefs in Transcendentalism and civil disobedience and was a dedicated abolitionist.

One of America's most famous writers, Henry David Thoreau is remembered for his philosophical and naturalist writings. He was born and raised in Concord, Massachusetts, along with his older siblings John and Helen and younger sister Sophia. His father operated a local pencil factory, and his mother rented out parts of the family's home to boarders.

A bright student, Thoreau eventually went to Harvard College (now Harvard University). There he studied Greek and Latin as well as German. According to some reports, Thoreau had to take a break from his schooling for a time because of illness. He graduated from college in 1837 and struggled with what do to next. At the time, an educated man like Thoreau might pursue a career in law or medicine or in the church. Other college graduates went into education, a path he briefly followed. With his brother John, he set up a school in 1838. The venture collapsed a few years later after John became ill. Thoreau then went to work for his father for a time.

After college, Thoreau befriended writer and fellow Concord resident Ralph Waldo Emerson. Through Emerson, he became exposed to Transcendentalism, a school of thought that emphasized the importance of empirical thinking and of spiritual matters over the physical world. It encouraged scientific inquiry and observation. Thoreau came to know many of the movement's leading figures, including Bronson Alcott and Margaret Fuller.

Emerson acted as a mentor to Thoreau and supported him in many ways. For a time, Thoreau lived with Emerson as a caretaker for his home. Emerson also used his influence to promote Thoreau's literary efforts. Some of Thoreau's first works were published in The Dial, a Transcendentalist magazine. And Emerson gave Thoreau access to the lands that would inspire one of his greatest works.

In 1845, Thoreau built a small home for himself on Walden Pond, on property owned by Emerson. He spent more than two years there. Seeking a simpler type of life, Thoreau flipped the standard routine of the times. He experimented with working as little as possible rather than engage in the pattern of six days on with one day off. Sometimes Thoreau worked as a land surveyor or in the pencil factory. He felt that this new approach helped him avoid the misery he saw around him. "The mass of men lead lives of quiet desperation," Thoreau once wrote.

His schedule gave him plenty of time to devote to his philosophical and literary interests. Thoreau worked on A Week on the Concord and Merrimack Rivers (1849). The book drew from a boating trip he took with his brother John in 1839. Thoreau eventually started writing about his Walden Pond experiment as well. Many were curious about his revolutionary lifestyle, and this interest provided the creative spark for a collection of essays. Published in 1854, Walden; or, Life in the Woods espoused living a life close to nature. The book was a modest success, but it wasn't until much later that the book reached a larger audience. Over the years, Walden has inspired and informed the work of naturalists, environmentalists and writers.

While living at Walden Pond, Thoreau also had an encounter with the law. He spent a night in jail after refusing to pay a poll tax. This experience led him to write one of his best-known and most influential essays, "Civil Disobedience" (also known as "Resistance to Civil Government"). Thoreau held deeply felt political views, opposing slavery and the Mexican-American War. He made a strong case for acting on one's individual conscience and not blindly following laws and government policy. "The only obligation which I have a right to assume is to do at any time what I think right," he wrote.

Since its publication in 1849, "Civil Disobedience" has inspired many leaders of protest movements around the world. This non-violent approach to political and social resistance has influenced American civil rights movement activist Martin Luther King Jr. and Mohandas Gandhi, who helped India win independence from Great Britain, among many others.

After leaving Walden Pond, Thoreau spent some time looking after Emerson's house while he was on tour in England. Still fascinated with nature, Thoreau wrote down his observations on plant and wildlife in his native Concord and on his journeys. He visited the woods of Maine and the shoreline of Cape Cod several times.

Thoreau also remained a devoted abolitionist until the end of his life. To support his cause, he wrote several works, including the 1854 essay "Slavery in Massachusetts." Thoreau also took a brave stand for Captain John Brown, a radical abolitionist who led an uprising against slavery in Virginia. He and his supporters raided a federal arsenal in Harpers Ferry to arm themselves in October 1859, but their plan was thwarted. An injured Brown was later convicted of treason and put to death for his crime. Thoreau rose to defend him with the speech "A Plea for Capt. John Brown," calling him "an angel of light" and "the bravest and humanest man in all the country."

In his later years, Thoreau battled an illness that had plagued him for decades. He had tuberculosis, which he had contracted decades earlier. To restore his health, Thoreau went to Minnesota in 1861, but the trip didn't improve his condition. He finally succumbed to the disease on May 6, 1862. Thoreau was heralded as "an original thinker" and "a man of simple tastes, hardy habits, and of preternatural powers of observation" in some of his obituaries.

While other writers from his time have faded into obscurity, Thoreau has endured because so much of what he wrote about is still relevant today. His writings on government were revolutionary, with some calling him an early anarchist. Thoreau's studies of nature were equally radical in their own way, earning him the moniker of "father of environmentalism." And his major work, Walden, has offered up an interesting antidote to living in the modern rat race.

Printed in Great Britain
by Amazon

4f000f10-5cd1-4539-9d41-48a92d128224R01